T0296046

Sustainable Energy Transition in South Asia

Challenges and Opportunities

Sustainable Energy Transition in South Asia

Challenges and Opportunities

Editors

S Narayan
Christopher Len
Roshni Kapur

National University of Singapore, Singapore

 **World Scientific**

NEW JERSEY · LONDON · SINGAPORE · BEIJING · SHANGHAI · HONG KONG · TAIPEI · CHENNAI · TOKYO

Published by

World Scientific Publishing Co. Pte. Ltd.
5 Toh Tuck Link, Singapore 596224
USA office: 27 Warren Street, Suite 401-402, Hackensack, NJ 07601
UK office: 57 Shelton Street, Covent Garden, London WC2H 9HE

Library of Congress Cataloging-in-Publication Data
Names: Kapur, Roshni, editor. | Narayan, S., 1943- editor. | Len, Christopher, editor.
Title: Sustainable energy transition in South Asia : challenges and opportunities /
    edited by S. Narayan (National University of Singapore),
    Christopher Len (National University of Singapore),
    Roshni Kapur (National University of Singapore).
Description: New Jersey World Scientific, [2019] | Includes bibliographical references and index.
Identifiers: LCCN 2019013309 | ISBN 9789811204319
Subjects: LCSH: Energy development--South Asia. | Renewable energy sources--South Asia. |
    Energy policy--South Asia.
Classification: LCC HD9502.S642 S87 2019 | DDC 333.79/40954--dc23
LC record available at https://lccn.loc.gov/2019013309

British Library Cataloguing-in-Publication Data
A catalogue record for this book is available from the British Library.

Cover design: Christopher Len

For any available supplementary material, please visit
https://www.worldscientific.com/worldscibooks/10.1142/11385#t=suppl

Desk Editor: Shreya Gopi

Typeset by Stallion Press
Email: enquiries@stallionpress.com

Contents

About the Contributors

Editors:

S. Narayan is a Visiting Senior Research Fellow at Institute of South Asian Studies (ISAS) at the National University of Singapore (NUS), Singapore. He has nearly four decades (1965–2004) in Public Service in the State and Central Governments, in Development Administration, was the Economic Adviser to the Prime Minister during 2003–2004. Prior to this assignment, Dr Narayan served the Government of India as Finance and Economic Affairs Secretary, Secretary in the Departments of Revenue, Petroleum and Industrial Development. As Secretary, Petroleum and Natural Gas, he was responsible for policy formulation and implementation in the hydrocarbon sector. Between 2000 and 2003, in the Ministry of Finance, his responsibilities included formulation of macroeconomic policy for the Government, tariff and taxation policies as well as initiatives for modernizing the capital markets. His special interests include public finance, energy policy, governance issues and international trade.

Dr Narayan obtained his PhD from the Indian Institute of Technology in New Delhi. He has an MPhil (Development Economics) from Cambridge University and Master of Business Management (Finance) from the University of Adelaide. He graduated with an MSc (Physics) from the University of Madras (Madras Christian College). Dr Narayan has single-authored one book, edited two books and written numerous policy papers, reports and book chapters. He also writes regularly in newspapers, both locally and internationally on issues relating to Public Policy, Governance, Public Finance, Trade and Energy. Dr Narayan has been a Visiting Senior Research Fellow at ISAS since 2005. After nine successful years as Head of Research at ISAS, Dr Narayan handed over the portfolio in mid-2014.

Christopher Len is a Senior Research Fellow and Head of Publications at Energy Studies Institute (ESI) at the National University of Singapore (NUS), Singapore. He obtained his PhD from the Centre for Energy, Petroleum and Mineral Law and Policy (CEPMLP) at the University of Dundee in Scotland. He also has degrees from the University of Edinburgh, Scotland and Uppsala University, Sweden.

He is also an Associate Fellow at the ISEAS-Yusof Ishak Institute in Singapore. He was previously a Research Fellow at the Stockholm-based Institute for Security and Development Policy (ISDP) where he was responsible for the Energy and Security in Asia Project. There, he also served as Executive Editor of the *China and Eurasia Forum Quarterly* journal published by the Central Asia-Caucasus Institute and Silk Road Studies Programme, which is a Joint Transatlantic Research and Policy Center affiliated with the Paul H. Nitze School of Advanced International Studies of Johns Hopkins University and ISDP. Len was also a Visiting Associate under the Energy Programme of the Institute of Southeast Asian Studies (ISEAS) in Singapore between 2006 and 2012. His research interests include Asia energy and maritime security, Chinese foreign policy, Arctic energy security and sustainable development, and the growing political and economic linkages between the various Asian sub-regions.

Roshni Kapur is a Research Analyst at the Institute of South Asian Studies (ISAS) at the National University of Singapore (NUS), Singapore. She graduated with a Master degree in Peace and Conflict Studies from the University of Sydney. She holds a Bachelor degree (with Honours) in Sociology with Law, from the University of London. Prior to joining ISAS, Roshni worked with the Singapore Committee for UN Women on public education initiatives with Mastercard. She has also worked as a digital journalist in HRM Asia. Her research focuses on post-war reconciliation, transitional justice, human rights and democratisation, food security and migration.

Contributors:

Mirza Sadaqat Huda is a Postdoctoral Fellow at School of Social Sciences, Nanyang Technological University (NTU), Singapore. His main interest is on multilateral cooperation on energy, water and the environment. He is also interested in evaluating the "spill over" effects of such cooperation on conflict resolution. Prior to his role at NTU, Mirza was a Research Analyst at the Sustainable Minerals Institute of the University of Queensland. He also worked as a Teaching Fellow at the Griffith Asia Institute of Griffith University. Mirza's peer-reviewed journal articles have been published in Geoforum, Energy Policy, Water International, Energy Research and Social Science and Strategic Analysis. He has a PhD from the University of Queensland, a Master of Security Studies from Macquarie University and a Bachelor of Commerce from the University of Canberra.

Syed Munir Khasru holds an MBA from the Wharton School of Business, University of Pennsylvania. He is Chairman of the international think tank, the Institute for Policy, Advocacy and Governance (IPAG). His expertise includes international relations and strategic affairs, regional connectivity and trade, energy and power. Khasru is experienced in multi-stakeholder dialogue in international platforms, including the World Economic Forum and G20. He provides policy recommendations to government and multilateral agencies. In the energy sector, he is a well-respected strategic thinker and policy analyst. He is a Member of the Asian Development Bank's Energy Leaders' Forum and gives advice on strategic issues and policy matters. He writes for leading international media outlets which include Project Syndicate, *Straits Times* (Singapore), *Nikkei Asian Review* (Japan), *South China Morning Post* (Hong Kong) and *The Hindu*.

Thusitha Sugathapala is a Senior Lecturer in Mechanical Engineering of the University of Moratuwa Sri Lanka; and a Chartered Engineer. Presently he is also performing duties as the Chairman — Intellectual Property Advisory Committee and the Director — Enterprise of the University of Moratuwa. He obtained the BSc Engineering Degree from University of Moratuwa and PhD from University of Cambridge. He served as the Head of the Department of Mechanical Engineering from 2005 to 2008, and the Director General of Sri Lanka Sustainable Energy Authority from 2011 to 2015. Dr Sugathapala's research areas of interest cover both energy and environment fields, including renewable energy; energy efficiency; and air quality management. He has been involved with development of policies and regulations including Renewable Energy Feed-in Tariff, Energy Efficiency, Clean Air 2025 Action Plan, Fuel Quality Road Map, Vehicle Emission Regulations, Stationary Sources Emission Standards and Nationally Determined Contributions (NDCs) in Power and Transport Sectors. He has also served as consultant to several national and regional programmes of the Asian Development Bank, World Bank, UNDP and UNEP.

Riasat Noor is the Head of Research and Publication at the Institute for Policy, Advocacy and Governance (IPAG). He is a research-savvy professional with experience in a wide spare of power and energy verticals and expertise in quantitative and qualitative analysis. He leads IPAG's power and energy projects, with work in energy value chain, sustainability reporting and investment in the energy sector. Currently, he is developing a "Power Sector Investability Index" for the Government of Bangladesh as well as potential investors to provide a guidance mechanism on an enabling policy and regulatory framework. A seasoned copy editor, Mr Noor has authored several publications on energy connectivity and digitisation, and appeared in platforms such as MIT Climate, UNIDO, the Economist Intelligence Unit, GSCASS, the Eurasian Forum (YES-Forum) and the APEC Energy Working Group. He also specializes in market research and multi-country survey and speaks widely on CCS and carbon pricing, CBET, and marine geopolitics, as well as advocates for energy security. Mr Noor has an MBA from the Institute of Business Administration (IBA), University of Dhaka, and has also worked with ILO and Nielsen Bangladesh.

Nitya Nanda is a research professional with more than two decades of experience in research, consulting and teaching in international trade, investment, environment and development issues, the political economy and the legal aspects of these in particular. His work covered issues and challenges in India, South Asia but often Southeast Asian and African nations as well. He has been involved with about 40 research/consulting projects, and in about half of them as the principal investigator. Currently, he is a Senior Fellow with The Energy and Resources Institute (TERI), India where he is also the Associate Director and Head of the Centre for Resource Efficiency and Governance. He has more than 120 research publications including nine articles in peer-reviewed journals, 30 in other journals, 35 book chapters in edited volumes, 28 monographs/briefing papers and 12 conference papers. He has authored two books and also edited four volumes. He has written several articles for newspapers and magazines. Currently, he is also the editor of TERI's flagship academic journal, *Journal of Resources, Energy and Development.*

Vikram Singh Mehta is an Executive Chairman of Brookings India and a Senior Fellow at the Brookings Institution, USA. Mr Mehta started his career with the Indian Administrative Service in 1978. He resigned in 1980 to join Phillips Petroleum in London as their senior economist. In 1984, he returned to India to join the government company Oil India Ltd. as an advisor for strategic planning. He joined Shell International in London in 1988. He was appointed managing director of Shell Markets and Shell Chemical Companies in Egypt in 1991, and chairman of the Shell Group of Companies in India in 1994.

Lydia Powell has been with the Observer Research Foundation, India for over 16 years working on policy issues in energy, water and the environment in the Indian context. Her current interests include energy security, energy access, carbon constraints and its impact on India's energy security, clean coal for energy and environmental security, regional cooperation for environmental security (India and Bangladesh) and Federalism and its impact on Indian energy policy. She contributes commentary and analysis on the Indian energy sector regularly. Her most recent paper was a book chapter on India's Energy Transitions. Ms Powell has also worked for

Norsk Hydro and for Orkla, two of Norway's largest conglomerates whose interests include energy. Ms Powell has three Post Graduate Degrees — two on Energy from Norway and one in Solid State Physics from India.

Amitendu Palit is a Senior Research Fellow and Research Lead (Trade and Economic Policy) at the Institute of South Asian Studies (ISAS) at the National University of Singapore (NUS), Singapore. He is an economist specializing in international trade policies, regional economic developments, comparative economic studies and political economy of public policies. He worked with the Government of India for several years with his longest span being in the Department of Economic Affairs in the Ministry of Finance, India.

Prior to joining ISAS in April 2008, he was with the Indian Council for Research on International Economic Relations (ICRIER), a leading economic policy research institute and think tank in Delhi. His current research focuses on economic and political implications of India's integration with the Asia-Pacific region, impact of mega-regional trade agreements, and various determinants of external trade and integration policies of China and India. His books include *The Trans Pacific Partnership, China and India: Economic and Political Implications* (2014; Routledge UK), *China India Economics: Challenges, Competition and Collaboration* (2011; Routledge) and *Special Economic Zones in India: Myths and Realities* (2008; Anthem Press; coauthored). He has also edited several books and published in peer-reviewed academic journals. He is a columnist for India's well-known financial daily, *Financial Express* and a regular contributor for the *China Daily*. He appears regularly as an expert on the BBC, Bloomberg, Channel News Asia, CNBC, Australian Broadcasting Corporation (ABC), Doordarshan (India) and All-India Radio.

Chapter 1

Introduction

S. Narayan, Christopher Len and Roshni Kapur

This edited volume is an outcome from the ESI-ISAS workshop titled "South Asia's Challenges and Opportunities in Sustainable Energy Transitions" held on 27 November 2017 and a half day conference titled "Towards a Low Carbon Asia: The Challenges of Ensuring Efficient and Sustainable Energy" on 28 November 2017.

This book consists of papers from a range of authors with varying backgrounds. It extensively covers a range of subjects on energy demand, energy security, regional energy cooperation, energy transition, cross-border electricity, renewable sources of energy and climate change. For this publication, we adopt the definition of the International Renewable Energy Agency (IRENA) which refers to energy transition as "a pathway toward transformation of the global energy sector from fossil based to zero-carbon by the second half of this century".[1]

South Asia's energy transition is a topic of growing interest. The region is home to a fifth of the world's population and undergoing rapid economic growth.[2] With the appropriate set of policies and reforms, South Asia has the capability to reach greater heights of development and prosperity. As the region grows economically, the demand for energy is increasing each year. According to the US Energy Information Administration (EIA), India was the third largest energy consumer in the world in 2013. In addition, EIA pointed out that after the United States, China and Japan, India was the fourth-largest consumer of crude oil and petroleum products, and also ranked as the fourth-largest net importer of crude oil and petroleum products.[3] As a major global energy consumer and importer, India is expected to have a growing impact on the global energy landscape as its energy consumption continues to increase.

In the lead up to the workshop and conference in 2017 and as this volume was being prepared in 2018, we have witnessed a fast evolving global energy landscape. Notable developments include the entering into force of the United Nations Framework Convention on Climate Change (UNFCCC) Paris Agreement in November 2016, US President Donald Trump's subsequent decision to pull the US from the Paris Agreement, the decision by OPEC and non-OPEC producers such as Russia to cut oil production in 2017 which later extended to the end of 2018, and the reinstating of US sanctions against Iran in November 2018. As these international events unfold, the key factors shaping South Asia's energy transition landscape have remained consistent; namely, the high level of fossil fuel dependence and the requirement to move the region towards more sustainable energy solutions.

Aim of the Book

With this book, we seek to address the following central question: How will the major economies of South Asia meet their growing energy demand? A number of related questions follow suit: How can the states diversify their energy consumption profiles and import sources? How will South Asia balance its commitment to reduce carbon emissions along with their investments in renewables? Can South Asia move towards a full-fledged renewable energy model? What are the opportunities and bottlenecks towards regional energy cooperation? What policy changes are required to overcome the challenges for both bilateral and multilateral energy engagements?

Each South Asian country needs to find a long-term and sustainable solution to meeting energy demand. At the same time, the states need to work collectively towards regional energy efficiency and the adoption of new renewable energy sources. While initial investments in renewable energy projects will take time to materialise, the long-term benefits are plenty. Greater energy connectivity in this region can also facilitate a new phase of regional cooperation.

Overview of the Chapters

This volume is divided into two sections with the regional section covering energy transition trends across South Asia, while the section on India examines the energy transition policies, strategies and challenges the country faces. In both sections, the authors cover a range of themes related to energy demand, energy security, regional energy cooperation, energy transition, cross-border electricity, renewable energy development and climate change.

The regional section begins with S Narayan's chapter which looks at the energy issues in India, Pakistan and Bangladesh. He details an individual case study of each country's strengths in energy resources, alternative sources for energy and options to adopt renewables and nuclear energy. All three countries are major importers of fossil fuels where they will need to look for new strategies to meet their growing energy consumption. However, the focus on renewables and nuclear energy will need to complement the existing power sources.

It then moves to Mirza Sadaqat Huda's analysis on the challenges to regional energy cooperation. He identifies the bilateral and regional energy projects in the region such as Turkmenistan–Afghanistan–Pakistan–India (TAPI) gas pipeline, Central Asia–South Asia (CASA-1000) and Turkmenistan–Uzbekistan–Tajikistan–Afghanistan–Pakistan (TUTAP) projects. Using literature review and interview data, he illustrates the key challenges and policy recommendations that may increase the probability of regional energy cooperation. Many of the interviewees have said that strong leadership by India could pave way for regional energy projects.

The following chapter by Syed Munir Khasru argues that energy connectivity and trading can be a game changer to forge greater integration among the states. He explores the impediments to regional connectivity such as non-trade barriers, copious amount of time for border clearance, inefficient seaport facilities and complex rules of origin. Bilateral trade on electricity and petroleum products trading is limited too. Khasru looks at these existing power trading agreements and provides policy recommendations on how to enhance regional cooperation. One key recommendation is to establish a centralised structure for a power agreement to connect the existing power exchanges platforms with operational adaptations.

Thusitha Sugathapala then looks at the potential for renewable energy in the region. He contends that not only technical and financial factors but also environmental and social factors affect the utilisation of renewable resources. He also looks at the drivers and challenges for renewable energy development in the region. The development of renewable energy technologies will reap multiple benefits such as job creation and business opportunities for the local population and the growth of the renewable energy sector will have an imprint on the bigger cross-section of the society.

Riasat Noor's chapter following on analyses the gaps in each country's energy supply and the existing trade in the region. The signing of the South Asian Association for Regional Cooperation (SAARC) agreement and development of the Bangladesh, Bhutan, India, Nepal (BBIN) network on energy collaboration were two hallmarks for energy trading but their scope is limited. On a bilateral level, India exports electricity to Bangladesh, Nepal and Bhutan but the power trading is limited too. He thinks that the energy trade if realised can be a game changer for South Asia since the region has enormous untapped and unutilised energy potential that can be optimised if institutional, political and technical barriers are addressed.

The last chapter in this section by Nitya Nanda makes a strong case for regional cooperation on energy issues. While some level of engagement has taken place, there is room for greater discourse to combat climate change. Cooperation has been initiated during expert meetings which led to the adoption of a three-year regional action plan in 2008. He proposed exploring the possibility of regional cooperation in adaptation and mitigation areas. Challenges exist though as some countries have set preconditions, while others have flagged the need for external assistance to reduce their mitigation costs.

The following section focuses on India's energy issues profile. It starts with Vikram Mehta's case study on India's energy profile in the long-run. He explores factors that will shape the country's energy profile and argues that the country shift towards a low carbon energy system if necessary. Despite India's interest in investing in renewable energy, fossil fuels will make up 77% of the country's energy requirements in 2040. As a result, non-renewable energy will continue to serve as the base for India's energy system.

Lydia Powell then examines the energy access transition in India and how biomass such as wood and agricultural products will gradually be replaced with petroleum products. However, there are contestations on the shift from biomass to petroleum projects. The chapter also explores the past and present day market transition.

Finally, Amitendu Palit's chapter examines the challenges of financing renewable and non-fossil fuel projects in India, with a primary focus on solar energy development. Early investments in renewable energy projects take time to materialise and bring in returns. He looks at the early days of India's journey to increase solar energy projects, the progress made and future trends. The green bond market in India has grown substantially to include commercial banks, financial institutions and corporates and this chapter explores India's approach towards clean energy finance through green bonds.

This volume ends with a closing chapter by Christopher Len and Roshni Kapur which highlight the key issues covered in this volume and offers some concluding thoughts on South Asia's energy transition path ahead.

End Notes

1. Energy Transition, International Renewable Energy Agency (IRENA), available on IRENA website: https://www.irena.org/energytransition https://www.irena.org/energytransition, accessed December 10, 2018.
2. "South Asia positioned to remain the world's fastest-growing region: UN report", United Nations Information Centre for India and Bhutan,

December 12, 2017, http://www.unic.org.in/pressrooms/south-asia-positioned-to-remain-the-worlds-fastest-growing-region-un-report/, accessed December 10, 2018.

3. India, US Energy Information Administration, June 14, 2016, https://www.eia.gov/beta/international/analysis.php?iso=IND, accessed December 1, 2018.

Section 1
South Asia

Chapter 2

Energy Demand in South Asia: Implications for the Future

S. Narayan

Introduction

The global energy scene in 2017 is fascinating in terms of the different strategies and actions across countries that are likely to determine energy mix, energy use, and the economics of energy in the world. Oil prices have ruled high through most of the year, beginning with the OPEC agreement on management of production, and exacerbated by the US stance on Iran. Problems in Venezuela and Nigeria have added to uncertainties in the output prices for oil. China's quest for reduction of coal consumption has dampened coal prices and coal trade in much of the world, and there is a renewed emphasis on renewable fuels for generation and transportation. Solar panel prices have been falling across the world and power costs from solar energy are fast approaching conventional fossil fuel-based power costs.

The year 2017 was significant in terms of energy demand. Global energy demand grew by 2.2% in 2017, up from 1.2% last year and above its 10-year average of 1.7%.[1] While the increase could be related to a pick-up in economic growth, it also reflected the improvement in energy intensity of production, that is, the amount of energy needed to produce one unit of output.

The vast majority of the increase in global energy consumption came from the developing world, accounting for 80% of the expansion. Energy consumption in China grew by over 3% in 2017, much faster than in the earlier 3 years.[2] There was a rebound in the production in the energy intensive sectors, namely iron, crude and non-ferrous metals. However, there was significant drop in energy intensity. Almost 60% of the increase in primary energy was provided by natural gas and renewable energy.[3] Natural gas (3.0%, 83Mtoe) provided the single largest contributor to the growth, followed by bio fuels and renewable energy.[4] The increase in coal consumption was driven by India, and to a lesser extent, China.

These developments have a profound effect on South Asia, with India, Pakistan and Bangladesh coping with this rapidly changing environment. The common feature of these three large economies of South Asia are that they are significant importers of fossil fuels. India imports over 80% of its annual oil needs, and while it has significant refinery capacity to be able to export refined products, the net costs of imports of close to 100 million tons of crude every year are quite significant for the economy. Pakistan and Bangladesh are also significantly dependent on oil imports, to the tune of 80% of their requirements. Power generation in Bangladesh was dependent on gas, but there are indications that the gas supplies would last less than two decades. With GDP growth in excess of 5% in all the three countries, energy demand is likely to grow rapidly in the next 10 years. It is not a surprise that the three countries are scrambling for strategies to ensure energy and fuel availability for their growth, and the quest spans technologies, politics and commerce. This paper is an attempt to look at the initiatives that are underway in these countries and their implications.

In South Asia, robust economic growth saw increases in energy consumption as reflected in Table 1.

South Asia will witness a growing demand for energy. In the three major economies of India, Bangladesh and Pakistan, there is a considerable growth in energy consumption. As these three countries are major importers of primary energy, there are political and strategic implications

Table 1: Primary energy profiles of selected South Asian countries.

Total Primary Energy Supply (TPES) by source — 2015

Country	Unit	Primary & secondary	Natural gas	Coal	Nuclear	Hydro	Geothermal, solar, etc.	Biofuels and waste	Total
India	kilotonne of oil equivalent (ktoe)	206,193	43,210	378,914	9,750	11,872	4,827	196,353	851,119
Pakistan	kilotonne of oil equivalent (ktoe)	25,032	26,479	4,984	1,584	2,924	72	32,795	93,870
Bangladesh	kilotonne of oil equivalent (ktoe)	4,960	21,237	2,270	0	49	14	9,340	37,870
India	share in total	24.2%	5.1%	44.5%	1.1%	1.4%	0.6%	23.1%	100%
Pakistan	share in total	26.7%	28.2%	5.3%	1.7%	3.1%	0.1%	34.9%	100%
Bangladesh	share in total	13.1%	56.1%	6.0%	0.0%	0.1%	0.04%	24.7%	100%

Source: International Energy Agency.

Primary energy: Consumption — 2017

Country	Unit	Oil	Natural	Coal	Nuclear	Hydro-	Renewable	Total
India	Million tonnes oil equivalent	222.1	46.6	424.0	8.5	30.7	21.8	753.7
Pakistan	Million tonnes oil equivalent	29.2	35.0	7.1	1.8	7.0	0.8	80.9
Bangladesh	Million tonnes oil equivalent	7.5	22.9	2.3	—	0.2	0.1	33.0
Total World	Million tonnes oil equivalent	4,621.9	3,156.0	3,731.5	596.4	918.6	486.8	13,511.2

(Continued)

Table 1:   (Continued)

Country	Unit	Oil	Natural	Coal	Nuclear	Hydro-	Renewable	Total
Share in World Consumption								
India	%	4.8%	1.5%	11.4%	1.4%	3.3%	4.5%	5.6%
Pakistan	%	0.6%	1.1%	0.2%	0.3%	0.8%	0.2%	0.6%
Bangladesh	%	0.2%	0.7%	0.1%	—	0.0%	0.0%	0.2%
Total World	%	100.0%	100.0%	100.0%	100.0%	100.0%	100.0%	100.0%
Share by Fuel Type								
India	%	29.5%	6.2%	56.3%	1.1%	4.1%	2.9%	100%
Pakistan	%	36.1%	43.3%	8.8%	2.2%	8.7%	1.0 %	100%
Bangladesh	%	22.7%	69.4%	7.0%	—	0.6%	0.3%	100%
Total World	%	34.2%	23.4%	27.6%	4.4%	6.8%	3.6%	13,511

Source: BP Statistical Review of World Energy 2018.

to energy growth in these countries. At the political level, the approaches of the three countries are likely to be different. Pakistan can rely on Saudi Arabia to provide some security for its oil needs. It still has to look for gas and coal, and does not seem to have any long-term contracts lined up yet. Bangladesh is also in a similar position. In India, maintaining a relationship with the oil producing countries, negotiating the Iran issue and opening up to new sources like the USA appear to be the political approaches. At the strategic level, Pakistan and Bangladesh might be expecting that lower demand for China's own consumption will open up these supply sources for them. In India, it is clear that for both coal and natural gas, there is going to be greater dependence on the private sector to look after the sourcing.

India

Energy consumption

Energy consumption in India has almost doubled since 2000, and is likely to double again by 2025. Consumption of energy is still low, and though the population is 18% of global population, the energy consumption is only 6%.[5] The country faces the dual challenge of providing power supply to nearly 200 million people who are without electricity, while at the same time making power available to fuel economic growth, which has been in excess of 7% for over 3 years now.[6]

The approach to solving the problems have been multi-fold. Taking advantage of the fall in oil prices after 2014, there has been deregulation of diesel and petrol prices. LPG prices have also become subsidy free. Thus, all oil-based fuels are now subsidy free. There is considerable relief to budgetary expenditures as a result of these measures. However, keeping petroleum products out of the ambit of the new Goods and Services Act has resulted in taxes and levies by the central as well as state governments, resulting in a burden on retail pricing that the consumer has had to bear. Fuel prices at the retail outlet for both petrol and diesel are higher than they were when oil was at $100 per barrel. The consequence has been that consumer prices have risen as these high retail prices work their way into the consumer's pocket through higher transportation and logistics costs, and currently inflationary pressures are visible. The Reserve Bank of India has had to increase interest rates twice in 2017–2018 by 25 basis points each time.[7]

In short, the fiscal relief for the budget has not translated into relief for the consumer. As oil prices rise, this is likely to be two-pronged pressure on the Government. The central Government as well as the state Governments are reluctant to give up the tax revenues on oil products which constitute a significant proportion of their revenues. With vehicle sales healthy, and private incomes rising, the Governments see transportation fuel prices as a sure source of revenue buoyancy. On the other hand, keeping retail prices high continues to stoke inflation, and with employment growth subdued, is likely to affect the consuming power of households, leading to dissatisfaction. Such dissatisfaction, in a pre-election year, would not be something that the political parties in power would welcome.

There is also uncertainty about long-term supply of oil. India has been a major importer of oil from Iran, and the current US sanctions against Iran are threatening this source of supply as well as the India–Iran political relationship. India is back to dependence on traditional suppliers from the Gulf countries, and is trying to source oil from the US as well. India bought crude oil from the US for the first time in 2017. High oil prices will be a pressure on the current account, and consumer inflation will be a pressure on real growth.

India has large reserves of coal and power generated from coal-fired stations still accounts for over 60% of all power generation.[8] As energy consumption grows, coal will continue to be an important fuel. In 2017, India consumed an additional 27 million tons of coal, an increase of 4.8% over the previous year.[9] This contributed to the first increase in global coal consumption in 4 years. Coal is by far the most important fuel in the energy mix, but India's recent climate pledge underlined the country's commitment to a growing role for low carbon sources of energy, led by solar and wind power. India is set to contribute more than any other country to the projected rise in global energy demand, around one-quarter of the total: even so, energy demand per capita in 2040 is still 40% below the world average.[10]

The 2015 World Energy Outlook Report by the International Energy Agency[11] indicates India's total energy demand will more than double by

2030, propelled higher by an economy that is more than five times larger in 2040 and a demographic expansion that makes India the world's most populous country. With energy use declining in many developed countries and China entering a much less energy-intensive phase in its development, India is emerging as a major driving force in global trends. This makes India the largest source of growth in global coal use. Oil demand increases by more than in any other country, approaching 10 mb/d by 2040. India steps up its deployment of renewables, led by solar power, for which India becomes the world's second-largest market. Natural gas consumption also triples to 175 bcm (although, at 8% in 2040, it still plays a relatively limited role in the overall energy mix).[12]

Urbanisation and industrialisation

India is urbanising very quickly. There are already 55 cities with a population of 1 million or more, a number that is likely to double by 2040.[13] Urbanisation would lead to switch to modern fuels, both for transportation as well as domestic use. Commercial demand as well as household demand could climb steeply. Three-quarters of the projected increase in energy demand in residential buildings comes from urban areas, driving the sector's energy use away from solid biomass (two-thirds of the total today) and towards electricity and oil (45% and 15% of the 2040 total, respectively). There is an opportunity to improve energy efficiency and use through mandating energy efficiency in appliances, use of LED lights for public lighting and encouraging energy efficiency in homes. This could lead to a growth in the manufacture of such energy efficient devices, and adoption of new technologies to improve efficiency of energy use. The "Smart Cities" programme,[14] launched in 2015, puts a welcome emphasis on integrated planning and provision of urban services (including power, water, waste and mass transportation), although faces the considerable challenge of coordinated delivery across different branches and levels of government.

The 2015 WEO also noted that,

> *Industrial energy use is buoyed by substantial growth in output of steel, cement, bricks and other building materials, and by the expansion of domestic*

manufacturing encouraged by the "Make in India" initiative. An innovative efficiency certificate scheme helps to dampen demand growth in the energy-intensive industries; the task of raising awareness and financing efficiency improvements in other sectors (such as the brick industry, which consists of more than 100 000 small producers) is more difficult.[15]

Vehicle ownership is rising at a compounded annual growth rate of around 18%, and therefore demand for transportation fuels is also likely to increase rapidly, along with urbanisation. According to the World Energy Report, 'In the transport sector, adding more than 250 million passenger cars, 185 million two- and three-wheelers and 30 million trucks and vans to the vehicle stock by 2040 explains two-thirds of the rise in India's oil demand, mitigated only in part by new fuel efficiency standards. Energy use in industry is the largest among the end-use sectors, its share in final consumption rising above 50% by 2040.'[16]

Power generation

India's path to power its power system needs to almost quadruple in size by 2040 to catch up and keep pace with electricity demand that — boosted by rising incomes and new connections to the grid — increases at almost 5% per year. However, the power sector needs investments and reforms. Investments in improved transmission and delivery, improved logistics and better fuel efficiency of existing stations. Some of the coal-fired power plants have been set up in the eighties, and are in urgent need of renewal, as they use outdated, subcritical technologies. The 2015 WEO presented a stark challenge for India,

The situation varies from state to state, but stimulating the necessary grid strengthening and capacity additions requires pressing ahead with regulatory and tariff reform and a robust system of permitting and approvals for new projects. In the meantime, regular load-shedding in many parts of the country obliges those consumers who can afford it to invest in costly back-up options, and results in poor quality of service for those who cannot. Taking population growth into account as well as the high policy priority to achieve universal electricity access, India adds nearly 600 million new electricity consumers over the period to 2040.[17]

There is now a focus on renewables and nuclear, and by 2040, over half of the additions to generating capacity would be from non-coal sources. There is a commitment to keep coal-based generation to 50% or less of the total generation. Given the step rise in energy demand, this is an uphill task, and has to go hand in hand with modernising existing power stations as well as improvement in transmission and distribution efficiencies. The share of coal in the power generation mix falls from three-quarters to less than 60%, but coal-fired power still meets half of the increase in power generation. Coal production from domestic mines, both public and private, would be hard put to meet the growth in coal demand, and there is clear indication that imports of coal would grow significantly. Coal demand that is two-and-a-half-times higher than today by 2040 (although still only around half the projected level in China) is the main factor behind a large rise in India's energy-related CO_2 emissions. At a time when global coal production is peaking and investment in new coalmines is not happening, this increase in demand would be a challenge to meet. Meanwhile, crude imports could rise to 7.2 mb/d in 2040, sourced predominantly from the Middle East.[18] India's refinery capacity is projected to rise steadily and refinery output is increasingly directed to meet rising domestic demand.

Key challenges

Thus, India faces a multitude of challenges on the energy front. There is dependence on imports of oil, coal and natural gas, which will grow. This would pressure not just on the current account balance and foreign exchange resources, but also require foreign policy interventions to balance the energy sourcing. Only recently, India has started buying oil from the US This makes sense, as there is a trade surplus with US. There is a need to look at imported coal and natural gas supplies, and therefore to build friendships and alliances to make these sources reliable and stable.

Second, meeting India's energy needs requires a huge commitment of capital. The World Energy report estimates that India would require $2.8 trillion in investment in energy supply in our main scenario. Over 75% would go to the power sector. Mobilising cost-efficient investment at average levels of well above $100 billion per year is a constant challenge for

Indian policy at national and state levels, requiring effective coordination between multiple institutions and levels of government (the model of "cooperative federalism"), continued efforts to overhaul India's energy regulatory framework and to simplify an often complex business environment.

These are policy challenges as well as challenges of implementation. The fragmented nature of energy policy implementation, spread across different ministries and regulators, hampers the adoption of a holistic view.

Pakistan

In 2017, the average energy demand was around 19,000 MW, while power generation was only around 15,000 MW, leaving a deficit of 4,000 MW.[19] Two-thirds of the population do not have access to electricity. The International Energy Agency projects energy requirements to rise to 49,000 MW by 2025.[20]

Pakistan's economy grew by 5.8% in 2017–2018.[21] This has led to the increase in power demand, and a fury of construction of new power stations. Between 2013 and 2018, 39 power projects with a total capacity of 12,230 MW have been added, with a shift towards greater reliance on coal-fired power stations. The China–Pakistan Economic Corridor (CPEC) envisages investments up to $35 billion in the energy sector to be implemented through Independent Power Producers.[22] The target is to generate an additional 15 GW with these investments. Most of the large investments in this are on coal-fired power stations. The new power stations at Sahiwal and Port Qasim, built with Chinese aid, are both coal based, and coal imports are set to increase substantially. Current import levels of seven million metric tons are expected to triple by 2030.[23] There are concerns that Chinese investments would lead to greater dependence on coal as a source of fuel, apart from adding to the fiscal burden of debt repayments. It is interesting that at a time when China is reducing coal-based power generation within its own borders, a significant proportion of new power stations that it is building as a part of the Belt and Road Initiative are coal based. There is thus a paradox between environmental responsibility within its borders to contribution to increases in carbon emissions elsewhere.

For Pakistan, LNG imports, using two Floating Storage regasification facilities, have also increased and are used to supply fuel for power and fertiliser plants. Power consumption continues to be substantially in the household sector (51%) with industrial consumption at 25% and agriculture at 10%.[24] Meanwhile, Pakistan continues to be heavily dependent on oil imports, with 85% of the requirements imported. At this GDP growth rate, the oil import bills will double in a decade.

There is a new political dispensation in Pakistan, which has yet to announce its economic agenda. The budget continues to be stressed, with several economists expecting that Pakistan would need yet another quantum of IMF assistance. Pakistan has been to the IMF several times, and there are reports that it would have to seek IMF aid yet again. Energy policy in Pakistan would be intertwined with foreign policy as well as fiscal policy, and it remains to be seen whether its dependence on China would increase further.

Bangladesh

The Bangladesh economy is also showing a robust growth of close to 6% year-on-year since 2012. The demand for electricity has grown considerably in the last 6 years, at an annual rate of 11.2%. The share of population with access to electricity has increased from 55.2% in 2010 to 74% in 2015. The installed capacity in 2016–2017 was around 16 GW, with a generation of around 9.5 GW that year. Natural gas met almost 68% of the country's commercial use of energy. A total of 26 gas fields have been discovered up to June 2017 with a cumulative production of around 15 tmc of gas so far. The remaining resources are around 12.5 tcf. Oil reserves are around 13 million metric tons. The remaining resources of oil and gas are not sufficient for the massive expansion in energy requirements that the economy would be facing in the coming decades, and hence dependence on imports is likely to grow. There is also a target of increasing installed power generation capacity to 24,000 MW by 2021 and 40,000 MW by 2030.[25] This would require fuel. Current generation is 66.5% from gas-based stations and coal and liquid fuels account for around 23%. There is import of power of 8% from India.[26]

Planning for energy in Bangladesh, given robust GDP growth, is a challenging task. There is need for reliable and long-term access to fuel which includes oil, gas as well as coal. There is a focus on solar plants, and a distribution of generating capacity between the private and the public sectors. Significant investments and projects are planned for improving transmission and distribution, and a focus on energy efficiency and conservation to improve efficiency of energy use in industry, commercial spaces as well as for domestic consumption.

There are also plans to import power. Currently, 500 MW of power is being imported from India, since 2013, and this would be enhanced by another 500 MW once transmission and distribution capacity at the receiving end is improved. There is a feasibility study underway for importing up to 1,000 MW of hydropower from India. There are also plans to import 2,000 MW of power from Bhutan and also another 2,000 MW from Nepal. Bangladesh has also signed a memorandum of understanding with China to enhance cooperation in the power sector.[27] This memorandum covers the entire gamut of generation, distribution, energy efficiency as well as renewable energy. It envisages substantial investment by China in the creating of infrastructure for power, on commercial terms, in Bangladesh.

There is demand for increase in transportation fuels as well as gas for industry. Assuming that gas-based stations would contribute 60% of total power generated, the need to secure long-term availability of gas, either through pipelines or through alternate sources, becomes urgent.

The Bangladesh planning and finance[28] documents do not describe how this investment growth will be funded. While there is a current account surplus due to healthy exports from the textile sector and remittances, these alone may not be able to fund the long-term requirements that the energy growth scenario envisages.

Conclusion — South Asia's Overseas Reliance

The growing demand for energy in South Asia needs to be seen against the global energy scene. It is clear that India, Pakistan and Bangladesh face challenges in securing long-term fuel sources, whether oil or gas or coal. At the global level, oil demand is growing, primarily from the oil importing countries. In 2017, demand grew by round 1.7 million barrels a day,[29] significantly greater than the 10-year average growth. Oil prices have firmed up, not just due to OPEC agreements, but also due to uncertainties in accessing oil from Iran, as well as economic and political problems in Argentina and Nigeria. It is unlikely that that the prices of $40 or $50 a barrel would come back.[30]

For India, Pakistan and Bangladesh, this poses a challenge. The three countries are facing constraints of long-term sourcing as well as finance. Pakistan alone can depend on Saudi Arabia to help out with their oil needs, for all others, it would be a negotiated, government-to-government, commercial transaction. India is attempting to source oil from the United States for the first time. However, given the uncertainties in the geopolitical scene, none of the three countries have a long-term strategy for oil imports planned out and in place. In India, there is a significant private sector with huge refining capacity which sources oil from even difficult locations. Private refining capacity is 60 million tons per annum.[31] Even so, the need to feed the government owned refineries requires diplomatic as well as political acumen. There is also the problem of paying for oil. India is running a current account deficit, and so is Pakistan. Bangladesh's current account is supported by textile exports and worker remittances, but these are unlikely to bear the long-term burden of oil import costs.

The picture is similar in the case of gas as well. Availability of gas and the pricing of gas continue to be problems. In addition, China has been increasing gas consumption in its quest for environmental sustainability, and during 2017, China's demand for gas went up by 15%, amounting to over a third of global increase in gas consumption. Requirements of gas for Bangladesh, for power generation, and in Pakistan, for power and industrial uses are likely to grow at a compounded annual growth rate in excess of 15% a year.[32] In India, the recent approach to city gas distribution for domestic, commercial and small industry uses is likely to boost demand several times in a decade. Quite apart from gas for transportation, this will see demand in India rising steeply. The requirements of gas for South Asia would have to be accessed from a limited number of producing countries.

Sourcing long-term gas will be a problem for India and for Bangladesh, while Pakistan can continue to look for gas from the Tajikistan pipeline. At the diplomatic and foreign policy level, there is little evidence that

India is taking this up as a priority. This is probably due to the fact that the external affairs ministry and the petroleum ministry are not acting together on issues of energy security, with both lacking domain knowledge in the other's area. The recent auctions of city gas distribution rights seem to indicate that the Indian Government would like to allow the private sector to take over gas distribution. This would mean that the private sector would have to find and lock in sources of supply. While new LNG trains have been commissioned in Australia and US, there is no evidence of oversupply. There is also no evidence that Bangladesh, Pakistan and India are locking in to these new supplies through long-term contracts.

It is interesting that the Chinese initiatives are going to steeply increase coal consumption in Pakistan. While China is reducing coal consumed for power, its belt and road initiatives are setting up coal-fired stations in a number of countries — an interesting paradox. Pakistan will have to import coal, and so will India and Bangladesh in the coming years. While in India, the proportion of power generated from coal powered stations will start to decrease, this will not be the case in Pakistan and Bangladesh. This has implications for environmental sustainability and global warming. Again, the Indian approach appears to be to leave this in the hands of the private sector, with domestic production being reserved for public sector generating plants.

The countries in South Asia are trying to embrace renewable energy alternatives, with a focus on solar power generation as well as windmills. Solar power is being attempted for roof tops and off grid locations, as well as for large grid linked stations. The drawback is that in none of the countries, there is adequate R&D happening in either panel technology or storage systems. It is China that is forging ahead in the field of electric vehicles and storage batteries as well as new technologies for making solar power cheaper and more efficient. The steep growth in energy demand that is envisaged is unlikely to be met from renewables alone, and dependence on coal and oil will continue. South Asian countries are likely to remain price takers of energy as well as technology dependent, in the absence of adequate indigenous efforts.

An important concern, especially in India, is the ability to pay. While prices of solar power have fallen, prices of coal generated power continue to be high. Distribution and consumption are in the hands of State power utilities, whose ability to collect tariffs from consumers is very poor, and a number of these utilities are in financial distress. This is a problem that needs to be tackled before the entire energy system becomes financially viable.

Lastly, the dependence on oil for transportation will continue, and will actually increase. Electric vehicles for cars may become a possibility, but for air, ships, rail and freight, dependence on oil engines will continue. With growing prosperity in the South Asian countries, the dependence on imported oil will continue to grow, and neither renewables nor electric transportation will be able to reduce this pressure.

End Notes

1. *BP Statistical Review of World Energy* 2018 (London: June 2018), p. 3.
2. *Ibid.*, p. 3.
3. *Ibid.*, p. 3.
4. *Ibid.*, p. 3.
5. "India," *International Energy Agency*, https://www.iea.org/countries/india, accessed January 15, 2019.
6. *Ibid.*
7. *Ibid.*
8. *Ibid.*
9. *Ibid.*
10. *Ibid.*
11. *World Energy Outlook 2015* (Paris: International Energy Agency, 2015), p. 14.
12. *Ibid.*
13. *Ibid.*
14. "Strategy", Smart Cities Mission, Ministry of Housing and Urban Affairs, Government of India, April 12, 2017, http://smartcities.gov.in/content/innerpage/strategy.php, accessed August 5, 2018.
15. *World Energy Outlook 2015* (Paris: International Energy Agency, 2015), p. 14.
16. *Ibid.*
17 *Ibid.*, p. 13.
18. "Energy", Pakistan Economic Survey 2017–2018, Ministry of Finance, Government of Pakistan, 2018, p. 215, http://121.52.153.178:8080/xmlui/handle/123456789/16248, accessed August 5, 2018.
19. *Ibid.*, p. 210.
20. *Ibid.*, p. 210.

21. *Ibid.*, p. 210.
22. *Ibid.*, p. 210.
23. *Ibid.*, p. 210.
24. *Ibid.*, p. 210.
25. "Power and Energy", *Bangladesh Economic REVIEW 2017*, Economic Adviser's Wing, Finance Division, Ministry of Finance, Government of the People's Republic of Bangladesh, 2017, p. 142, https://mof.portal.gov.bd/sites/default/files/files/mof.portal.gov.bd/page/e8bc0eaa_463d_4cf9_b3be_26ab70a32a47/Ch-10%20(English-2017)_Final.pdf, accessed August 5, 2018.
26. *Ibid.*
27. *Ibid.*
28. Power and Energy", *Bangladesh Economic REVIEW 2017*, Economic Adviser's Wing, Finance Division, Ministry of Finance, Government of the People's Republic of Bangladesh, 2017, https://mof.portal.gov.bd/sites/default/files/files/mof.portal.gov.bd/page/e8bc0eaa_463d_4cf9_b3be_26ab70a32a47/Ch-10%20(English-2017)_Final.pdf, accessed August 5, 2018.
29. *BP Statistical Review of World Energy 2018* (London: June 2018), p. 3.
30. *Ibid.*
31. *Ibid.*
32. *Ibid.*

Chapter 3

Addressing Challenges to Regional Energy Cooperation in South Asia*

Mirza Sadaqat Huda

Introduction

South Asia is one of the most energy insecure regions in the world in addition to being extremely vulnerable to climate change. The region's energy challenges are underpinned by a complex set of interlinked issues which includes chronic energy shortages, dependence on costly imported hydrocarbons and constraints to renewable energy due to financial, behavioural and technical limitations. These issues need to be urgently addressed for the region to continue to grow while pervasive poverty is addressed.

Regional cooperation is potentially a sustainable and environmentally viable solution to the energy insecurity faced by South Asian countries. The basic rationale for regional energy cooperation is provided by a

*The findings of this book chapter are based on the author's PhD thesis, completed from the Sustainable Minerals Institute, The University of Queensland. The fieldwork for this research was funded by the Sustainable Minerals Institute. Sections three and four of this chapter draws heavily from the author's earlier work: Huda and McDonald (2016). Regional cooperation on energy in South Asia: Unraveling the political challenges in implementing transnational pipelines and electricity grids. *Energy Policy* 98, (November), 73–83.

mismatch between energy demand growth and energy resource endow-
ments. On the one hand, Turkmenistan, Iran, Nepal and Bhutan have
hydropower and hydrocarbon resources that are far in excess of their
energy demand. On the other hand, while India, Pakistan, Bangladesh
and Afghanistan have modest hydroelectric and natural gas resources,
their energy demand growth is buoyed by larger population and economies growing at a faster rate. In 2017, the primary energy consumption
growth rate was highest in Pakistan (6.1%), followed by India (4.6%) and
Bangladesh (3.6%).[1,34]

Despite the establishment of the economic and technical rationale of
regional energy projects within academic as well as policymaking circles,
not a single multilateral energy project has been implemented to date,
while bilateral cooperation remains limited. While valuable, the majority
of studies on regional energy cooperation have based the essence of their
analysis on why regional energy projects should be implemented. Very few
studies have attempted to explain the issues that have prevented multilateral energy projects and limited the scope of bilateral cooperation since
1947. While political challenges have been identified within existing studies as the primary impediment to energy cooperation,[2-4] there is a dearth
of analysis on the specific dimensions of these challenges beyond simplis-
tic references to India's territorial conflict with Pakistan. However, while
these studies have identified political issues as key impediments to cooperation, they have not undertaken extensive analyses of these challenges or
provided evidence to substantiate their assumptions. While the technical
and economic rationale of regional energy projects have been widely
accepted within political and academic circles, contemporary literature
does not give any explanation for the absence of multilateral energy projects and the limited number of bilateral projects.

To meet this gap, this chapter aims to undertake an analysis of the
challenges to regional energy cooperation in South Asia. Using interview
data with policymakers from India, Bangladesh, Pakistan and Nepal, it
highlights three broad challenges to energy cooperation: political challenges, security threats and environmental degradation. The chapter provides policy recommendations that can address these challenges and
enhance the prospects of energy integration in South Asia. To identify
political challenges to energy cooperation and explore remedial policy

options, this study draws on an extensive literature review as well as interviews with policymakers in South Asia. Literature review consisted of academic as well as institutional studies and project documents. From October 2014 to March 2015, the author undertook 45 semi-structured interviews with policymakers in India, Nepal, Pakistan and Bangladesh. The respondents included government officials, academics, representatives of regional institutions and officials of multilateral development banks. All the interviews were undertaken under conditions of anonymity. In addition to interviews, the fieldwork component of this study included 1–3 months Visiting Fellowships in think tanks in India and Nepal. After the data had been triangulated and analysed, the results were interpreted to provide answers to the research question.

This chapter has five sections. First section serves as introduction. Following on below, second section provides an overview of the current state of regional energy cooperation in South Asia. Third section consists of a detailed analysis of the obstacles to cooperation by uncovering various political, security and environmental challenges to energy cooperation. This is followed by the fourth and final section which contains the policy recommendations and the conclusion for this piece.

Energy Cooperation in South Asia: An Overview

To date, not a single multilateral energy project has been implemented in the region, and bilateral energy cooperation exists only between India and the smaller countries of Bangladesh, Bhutan and Nepal. The smaller countries of South Asia do not have any energy projects with each other. The current state of bilateral energy cooperation and an overview of proposed multilateral energy projects are outlined in the following.

India–Bangladesh: Before 2008, Bangladesh's conflict-prone relationship with India greatly undermined the prospects of energy cooperation. India and Bangladesh's cooperation on energy is a recent phenomenon and can largely be attributed to the bonhomie between the current ruling political parties in Dhaka and New Delhi.

The very first India–Bangladesh power project was a 500 MW cross-border transmission line between Bheramara and Baharampur which came online as recently as 2013. In addition, several bilateral projects are under construction or being planned. Steps are being undertaken to increase the capacity of the Bheramara–Baharampur line from 500 to 1,000 MW. In March 2016, a 100 MW power line that would transfer electricity from the Indian state of Tripura to Bangladesh was officially inaugurated. An India–Bangladesh friendship pipeline is being planned, which would allow up to 1 million metric tonnes of diesel import from India per year. The Bangladesh–India Friendship Power Company (Pvt.) a 50–50 joint venture between Bangladesh Power Development Board and India's National Thermal Power Corporation, is building a 1,320 MW coal-fired power plant near the Sundarbans, the world's largest mangrove forest.[5] Talks are also being undertaken on the construction of a 3,000 MW transmission line between the Indian states of Assam and Bihar through Bangladesh. Dhaka has been offered a proportion of the electricity as transit fee.[6]

India–Nepal: Despite the potential of trade in hydroelectricity, India's cooperation with Nepal has been constrained by mistrust, conflict and a historical sense of injustice. Nepalese mistrust of India has been reinforced by what it perceives as unequal treaties starting from the Sharada Dam (1927), Kosi Agreement (1954), Gandak Agreement (1959), Tanakpur Agreement (1991) and the Mahakali Treaty (1996).[7]

Despite many political hurdles, Indo-Nepal Power Exchange began in 1971 with the exchange of about 5 MW of power, and by 2001–2002, the exchange of power had grown to 100–150 MW.[8] Currently, projects being considered or planned include the 5,600 MW Mahakali Pancheswar Project and four cross-border electricity transmission lines, namely the Butwal–Gorakhpur, Duhabi–Purnea, Dhalkebar–Muzaffarpur and Anarmani–Siliguri. In 2015, Kathmandu and New Delhi signed an agreement to build an oil pipeline from the Indian state of Bihar to Amlekhgunj in Nepal. In August 2014, the two countries signed a bilateral Power Trade Agreement as well as power development agreements for two hydroelectric projects, the Upper Karnali and Arun III, each with a generation capacity of 900 MW.

India–Bhutan: Bhutan's energy cooperation with India is underpinned by the status of Thimphu as a protectorate of New Delhi. The Treaty of Friendship and Cooperation signed between the two countries required Bhutan to consult India on all matters related to foreign policy from

1949 to 2007. The Treaty has since been renegotiated, and Bhutan has expressed the desire for more control of its foreign policy.[9] However, India still exerts considerable influence in Bhutan.

The export of electricity from Bhutan is presently limited to India. Average annual generation from its five major hydropower plants is 7,865 GWh, and in 2007, total energy generation from these five hydro projects was 6,400.75 GWh. In 2007, Bhutan's total energy exported to India was 5,689 GWh. All the existing major hydropower projects, with the exception of Basochhu, were undertaken through assistance from India, with about 60% of the cost through grant and the remaining as soft loan. The pricing of electricity has been based on various issues including the grant component of funding, the cost of operation and maintenance and sustainability rather than any market driven mechanism.[10] The two countries plan to develop ten hydropower dams to generate around 11,576 MW by 2020.[11] At present, 3 of these projects, the 1,200 MW Punatsangchu-I, 1,020 MW Punatsangchu-II and 720 MW Mangdechhu are under construction, while the rest are in various stages of evaluation and negotiation.[12]

Afghanistan–Pakistan–Central Asia: To date, Afghanistan and Pakistan have not undertaken energy cooperation with each other or with any other country in South Asia. While substantial opportunities exist for collaboration on electricity between India and Pakistan,[13] significant political conflicts have prevented any cooperation from taking place. Afghanistan's lack of collaboration with the other countries of South Asia is mostly due to the ongoing insurgency in the country and the political conflicts between Islamabad and Kabul.

In 2015, 78% of total consumed electricity in Afghanistan was imported from neighbouring Tajikistan, Turkmenistan, Uzbekistan and Iran. In addition, Afghanistan imports 10,000 tonnes of refined oil every day from Turkmenistan, Uzbekistan, Russia and Iran.[14] At present, Pakistan is importing 40 MW of electricity from Iran. In February 2007, the countries signed a contract for the supply of 100 MW of power from Polan, Iran to Gwadar, Pakistan. A Memorandum of Understanding has been signed between the two countries to conduct a feasibility study for importing 1,000 MW of power from Iran. The 1,800 km Iran–Pakistan pipeline is expected to be completed in 2018 and will transfer 21.5 million cubic metres of gas per day (mcm/d) from the South Pars gas field in Iran to Karachi in Pakistan.[15]

Besides the projects listed above, a number of multilateral energy projects in South Asia are being planned or have been proposed. This includes both pipeline and hydroelectric projects. Brief descriptions of these are as follows.

The Turkmenistan–Afghanistan–Pakistan–India Pipeline (TAPI): Officially inaugurated by the leaders of all four participating countries in December 2015, the TAPI aims to transfer gas from Turkmenistan's Galkynysh field (with a capacity of 16 trillion cubic feet) through Afghanistan to Pakistan and then into India. The ADB has been TAPI's secretariat since 2002 and has spearheaded the legal, institutional and technical aspects of the project. In 2014, the state gas companies of the four countries created the TAPI Pipeline Company, which aims to build, finance, own and operate the pipeline.[16] While the project was initially expected to be completed in 2019, construction of the pipeline has not yet started, and efforts are underway to attract funding.

The Central Asia–South Asia Power Project (CASA-1000): This project envisions the transfer of excess hydroelectricity from the Kyrgyz Republic and Tajikistan in the summer months, when there are massive shortages of power in Afghanistan and Pakistan. The project is slowly taking shape, particularly through the creation of a critical framework called the Inter-Governmental Council. Various initiatives are being undertaken in the realms of procurement of infrastructure and technology. In addition to the commitment of the four countries, CASA-1000 has the support of the World Bank, the Islamic Development Bank and USAID.[17]

The Turkmenistan–Uzbekistan–Tajikistan–Afghanistan–Pakistan electricity Project (TUTAP): The TUTAP project envisions transmission connections and hydroelectric trade between the three Central Asian countries of Turkmenistan, Uzbekistan and Tajikistan and the South Asian nations of Afghanistan and Pakistan. The project is supported by the ADB and progress is evident by the construction of transmission lines, of which the Tajikistan and Afghanistan component was completed in 2011, and the inclusion of the TUTAP within Afghanistan's Power Sector Master Plan of 2013.[18] As of February 2018, the ADB has undertaken projects to strengthen the energy sector in Afghanistan and framework agreements have been signed between Kabul, Islamabad and Ashgabat.[19]

Bangladesh–Bhutan–India–Nepal (BBIN): The BBIN aim to collectively harness the hydroelectric potential of the Ganges–Brahmaputra–Meghna (GBM) river basin that is shared by the four countries. So far, four meetings of BBIN have taken place, and various issues related to hydropower and water resources have been discussed.[20]

Although the brief overview of regional projects provided above may suggest that such efforts are steadily gathering momentum, the TAPI pipeline was originally proposed as far back as 1990.[21] Despite recent progress in negotiations, doubts have been raised about the completion of the project. Proposals to undertake multilateral cooperation on harnessing the hydropower potential of the GBM Basin have existed for decades[22] but these projects still remain in the discussion stage. In this context, it is important to examine the issues that impede energy cooperation in the region.

Obstacles to Cooperation

Political challenges

As mentioned earlier in this chapter, contemporary literature has consistently highlighted political issues as the biggest challenge to the energy cooperation but has not provided a systematic analysis of these issues. In the context of energy cooperation, political challenges have been attributed almost exclusively to geopolitical issues, such as India's historical preference for bilateralism, the Kashmir conflict and deep-set regional mistrust in South Asia. However, while such issues undoubtedly hinder collaboration, data collected through interviews has revealed that in addition to geopolitical conflicts, energy cooperation in South Asia is held back by the failure of political leadership in the realms of domestic consensus building, effective articulation of the benefits of regional cooperation and bridging gaps between key stakeholders, among others. These political challenges are as follows:

Domestic politics

Political leaders in the domestic arena have so far failed to synchronise their objectives with regional cooperation and have in various ways impeded the building of consensus on energy projects. In Bangladesh, the rivalry between the two major political parties, the Awami League (AL) and the Bangladesh Nationalist Party (BNP) has resulted in the foreign policy of Bangladesh being heavily politicised and unrepresentative of national consensus or national interests, which has proved to be a major impediment to the realization of regional energy projects. In the periods governed by the BNP, the bilateral relationship with India would be bitter, whereas under the AL-led government the bilateral relations would improve to such an extent that some would consider the relationship to be sycophantic. An Associate Professor at Jahangirnagar University in Dhaka has stated that energy cooperation in South Asia is greatly undermined by the domestic politics of Bangladesh, as any attempt by a particular administration to undertake cooperation with India is bound to be criticized by the opposition.

In Nepal, the consistent political instability that has followed the end of a decade-long civil war in 2006 has greatly undermined the country's ability to undertake regional cooperation. Constant feuding between Nepal's biggest political parties — The Communist Party of Nepal (Maoist-Centre) (CPN-MC), the Communist Party of Nepal (Unified Marxist–Leninist) (CPN-UML) and Nepali Congress (NC) has prevented the drafting of a constitution until September 2015. A former Research Fellow of the SAARC Energy Centre has stated in an interview that the political instability in Nepal has prevented the government from taking any steps towards regional energy cooperation. In similarity with Bangladesh, any cooperative ventures with India are subject to political rhetoric in Nepal.

The federal structure of India and the de-centralised nature of power make domestic actors in individual states a significant player in regional negotiations. Five states of India share an international border, and the role of domestic politics become particularly potent when negotiations are undertaken with a neighbouring country on issues such as water or energy. A case in point was the failure by the central government of India to reach an agreement with Bangladesh on the allocation of the Teesta River in 2011, due to opposition by the Chief Minister of the Indian state of West Bengal, Mamata Banerjee, who refused to accept the political implications that the agreement would have in her constituency. In addition to water, the disparity in objectives between the central government and the states of India has created barriers to energy cooperation. An Associate Fellow at the Energy and Resources Institute (TERI) stated that the contradiction of exporting energy when shortfalls exist in the domestic market is arguably one of the biggest political constraints to energy cooperation. The respondent revealed that that the 500 MW Baharampu–Bheramara transmission line between Bangladesh and India created some discontent in the state of West Bengal, with several media outlets questioning the validity of exporting energy when local demand is unfulfilled.

While the states of India can have an impact on regional cooperation, Delhi's attitude towards the states that border neighbouring countries can also create barriers to energy projects. A case in point is the lack of investment in the economically backwards and insurgency-prone Northeast Indian states, which border Bangladesh and has a reported hydroelectric capacity of 58,971 MW. Several analysts in Bangladesh and India have opined that successful cooperation on hydroelectricity between India, Nepal and Bangladesh is dependent on whether the Narendra Modi-led administration invests in the Northeast Indian states and undertakes policy measures to reduce the threat from insurgents. In addition, cross-border energy cooperation hinges on whether Indian politicians attempt to resolve the sensitive issue of Bangladeshi migrants in Northeast India from the perspective of ethno-nationalism or human rights.

Although the Kingdom of Bhutan is politically more stable than its neighbours, the national discourse puts great emphasis on the preservation of nature and Bhutan is unlikely to undertake regional cooperation at the cost of the environment, even if compensation is offered. The secluded nature of Bhutan and its adherence to the concept of gross national happiness, which has the conservation of nature as one of its four pillars, puts it greatly at odds with countries like India and Bangladesh that have followed a more conventional path of development, owing to demographic and other reasons.

Energy cooperation is also impeded by the actions of domestic political actors who gain from keeping the Indo-Pak conflict alive. In India, the BJP which assumed power in 2014 is affiliated to the Rashtriya Swayamsevak Sangh (RSS), a Hindu nationalist group. Organisations with similar ideologies such as the Shiv Sena have repeatedly undermined any peaceful overtures with Pakistan, including the disruption of sporting and cultural events and a similar response is expected in regard to energy cooperation. On the other hand, the Pakistani Army's meddling in domestic politics and the Pakistani establishment's open support to Hafeez Saeed, the alleged mastermind of the Mumbai terror attacks and other anti-India terrorist groups creates an environment where undertaking collaboration on energy projects seem impractical.

The politicisation of energy cooperation

In South Asia, resource nationalism is a fundamental challenge to regional energy cooperation.[23] However, the root cause of the rise of resource nationalism in South Asian countries is the fallacy of the way by which resources are conceptualised, accessed and communicated by politicians.

Firstly, energy resources are conceptualised by political leaders from a narrow-minded, proprietorial perspective. A Nepali expert on regional cooperation stated that the political leaders of the region often focus solely on the total amount of hydrocarbon deposits or hydroelectric potential in their jurisdiction, rather than attempt to create public consensus on the accumulated benefits of resource utilisation. This confined perception was apparent among certain political leaders in Bangladesh when Indian companies signed production sharing contracts with Dhaka to explore hydrocarbons in the Bay of Bengal in early 2014. Political rhetoric about the total value of hydrocarbon deposits or hydroelectric potential in individual countries by leaders perpetuates the perception of energy resources as a strategic asset that needs to be controlled rather than one that should be utilised for the betterment of mankind.

Secondly, politicians for the most part have failed to access the cost of non-cooperation on energy issues. One of the reasons for the lack of consensus on the cost of non-cooperation is the inherent link between energy and electoral politics in South Asia, which has created the acceptance of energy as a political good rather than an economic one. As stated by several interview respondents, calculating the cost of non-cooperation in the energy sector, particularly as it relates to the economy and environment of individual South Asian countries, may provide an important incentive towards greater energy cooperation.

Thirdly, energy cooperation in South Asia is held back by multiple failures by political leaders to effectively communicate with various stakeholders. Interview respondents have mentioned both the lack of messengers as well as the quality of the message as impediments to the wider acceptance of regional energy projects. Some respondents lamented the lack of spokespersons among the South Asian political leadership with the ability to galvanise regional consensus. Others stated that the narrative of energy cooperation itself requires improvement. A Research Fellow from the Observer Research Foundation (ORF) stated that politicians need to change the narrative of energy cooperation from that of energy trade at the state-to-state level, to one of energy access, electrification and poverty alleviation. Therefore, the lack of leaders who are willing to act as focal points for regional energy cooperation and have the ability to articulate the importance of such projects not just among the intelligentsia but also the common people is a significant barrier.

Politicians have also failed to communicate with researchers on important technical issues regarding energy cooperation. Technocrats are concerned with technical issues such as cost-benefit analysis, technical feasibility and pricing mechanism while politicians are mostly concerned about their electoral base and political manifestos. An economist from the International Centre for Integrated Mountain Development (ICIMOD) opined that due to this gap in professional objectives, researchers have failed to communicate findings in a way that it is appealing to the policymakers. The policymakers, on the other hand, have not put enough effort to grasp the various economic analyses put forward by the researchers, as their priorities have always been directed by populist agendas. The failure in communication between these two important actors in regional energy cooperation is thus a significant impediment to the realisation of energy projects.

Corruption

Several interview respondents have opined that the endemic corruption among the political and bureaucratic class in South Asia can undermine the feasibility of cross-border energy projects. A former member of the Governing Board of the SAARC Energy Centre stated that corrupt politicians may enable malpractice by multinational energy companies. If such corruption leads to social unrest, it can create a significant barrier to the realisation of energy projects. The respondent stated that Nigeria, which has become a case study in the "resource curse" theorem due to the collusion between multinational companies and corrupt political leaders, should be a cautionary tale for South Asia. Notwithstanding the significant contextual discrepancy between Nigeria and South Asia, the culture of impunity among South Asian politicians and the rather unscrupulous reputation garnered by some multinational energy companies, pose a significant barrier towards creating national consensus on the acceptance of regional energy projects.

Security challenges

Within literature on energy cooperation, security challenges to energy cooperation are only second to political issues in terms of in terms of intractability. Predominantly, these challenges consist of deliberate disruptions to energy supplies as a result of armed conflict and the threat posed by terrorist groups to energy infrastructure.[24,25] Several interview respondents, including a retired Indian Diplomat and a Pakistani security analyst stated that terrorists and insurgents in Afghanistan and Pakistan pose a significant threat to pipeline projects such as the TAPI. In addition, several Indian analysts mentioned that pipeline projects that traverse Pakistan and then into India are not feasible as New Delhi cannot allow Islamabad to have control on the latter's energy supplies. However, in addition to the importance of the security of physical infrastructure, the data collected through interviews has revealed that there are several other security issues related to regional energy projects, which while absent in contemporary literature, can pose as significant impediments. These gaps are outlined in the following:

Studies on regional energy cooperation in South Asia have mostly failed to address the socio-economic impact of transboundary energy projects on the millions of people who live in proximity to the crime and conflict-prone borders of the region.[26,27] A researcher at the Institute of Energy at Dhaka University stated that it is important to address the concerns, well-being and perceptions of local stakeholders where energy projects are being planned to be constructed. The populations that live across the region's arbitrary, haphazard borders are some of the most vulnerable and destitute people in the world.[28] Such borders are also rife with smuggling, piracy, terrorism, illegal immigration and the trafficking of drugs and humans. A 2013 report by Saferworld found that drug trafficking and transnational crime was driving insecurity and violence at the Bangladesh-Myanmar border.[29] Human rights violations committed by the Burmese Junta during the construction of the Yadana pipeline is an example of how large energy projects can have significant adverse impacts on communities if socio-economic issues are not factored in the planning of pipelines.[30] As stated by Ebinger[31] "both current and prospective energy trade will be influenced by disaffected populations in key areas of each country where energy production and transit corridors will be located".

Environmental challenges

Key informant interviews with policymakers in India, Bangladesh and Nepal have revealed a discrepancy in perceptions regarding the environmental impact of proposed multilateral hydroelectric projects. Hydroelectric dams are considered economically and environmentally desirable in Bangladesh and India with some policymakers referring to such projects as clean and free of environmental harm. Nepalese policymakers, while not undermining the economic benefits of hydroelectric projects have consistently highlighted the perceived negative impact of such ventures on the environment of the country. The respondents have also conveyed their frustrations with India's unwillingness to compensate Nepal for losses due to flooding. While perceptions about these projects in Bangladesh and India are influenced by the desire to benefit from the import of electricity, Nepalese views are informed by the fact that the actual construction of the dams would take place within their territory.

This discrepancy in the perception of environmental security between the country producing the hydroelectricity and those that import it can be a significant barrier to the realization of projects between India, Nepal and Bangladesh. This gap in perception also bears relevance to the hydroelectric projects being planned in the west of South Asia, namely the CASA-1000 and the TUTAP.

The analysis in the previous section has revealed a number of political, security and environmental challenges to regional energy cooperation in South Asia.

Recommendations and Conclusion

Recommendations: Addressing challenges to energy cooperation

Interviewees in all four countries have stressed the importance of political leadership to overcome the various impediments to energy projects. In particular, policymakers in India, Bangladesh and Nepal have expressed hope in the leadership of India's Narendra Modi due to his emphasis on enhancing regional cooperation and building ties with neighbouring countries. Political leadership, however, is a broad term and its particular role in alleviating the specific challenges to energy cooperation needs to be unravelled:

Articulation of a case for regional energy cooperation to the general public

From the challenges identified above, three particular recommendations regarding articulation of energy cooperation are provided. Firstly, the need to champion energy cooperation by the highest level of political leadership is required, building on the 18th SAARC Summit in 2014. Secondly, to gain acceptability of such projects among the wider masses, leaders must reiterate energy cooperation as a means to provide access to the underprivileged and as a facilitator of poverty alleviation. Thirdly, at the domestic level, leaders should stress the benefits that can be derived from resource utilisation as opposed to engaging in political rhetoric about the total value of resource deposits in a particular constituency. Such an articulation can potentially counter the widely held perception in South Asia that resources from a particular country should be used to ensure the energy security of the domestic population before being traded with a neighbouring state.

Building domestic consensus

Overcoming domestic political impediments to energy cooperation requires the building of consensus among political parties, which is extremely difficult. Politicians from the ruling parties of the region must undertake the difficult tasks of addressing any legitimate concerns that the opposition may have regarding the trade of energy with neighbouring states. However, it needs to be recognised that many political parties oppose projects simply for the sake of creating deadlocks and impeding progress. In this case, leaders must employ independent economists and environmental scientists to undertake transparent studies on the impact of energy projects. Ensuring access to information, freedom of media and an independent Environmental Impact Assessment can also build domestic consensus for energy projects. Studies by SAARC on the gains of regional cooperation to the individual countries of the region, with particular emphasis on the benefits to India can be instrumental in increasing domestic support for energy projects. Wider dissemination of these benefits among print and electronic media in South Asian countries can create domestic support for the inclusion of regional cooperation within the mandate of political parties in individual countries.

An important aspect of building domestic consensus for energy projects would be the containment of the activities of extremist groups in India and Pakistan. The propaganda being disseminated against Pakistan by Bangladeshi "secular" groups and against India by Nepali "nationalist" parties also requires moderation. However, these groups, rather than being peripheral minorities are very much part of the mainstream political forces in India, Bangladesh and Nepal and have close security–military ties in Pakistan. Whether leaders in South Asia will endanger their own political survival by trying to stop these spoilers from sabotaging cooperation remains a question.

Effective leadership by India

A majority of interviewees from the four countries have stated that astute leadership by India is essential to the realisation of regional energy projects. For energy projects to become a reality, India must move away from the practice of envisioning grand schemes of multilateral cooperation at regional forums while insisting on bilateralism at the policy-level. The need, therefore, is to create the necessary environment for cooperation to take place. This can be achieved if New Delhi provides land access to

Bangladesh to import electricity from Nepal and Bhutan. The creation of a regional hub in Siliguri, the small strip of Indian territory that separates Bangladesh, Nepal and Bhutan would have the necessary impact to stimulate a range of collaborative infrastructure and development projects, an opportunity that has been held back by parochial perspectives on territorial control. As has been suggested by a number of interviewees in all four countries, if India facilitates the successful development of energy cooperation in the eastern side of South Asia, it may make the difficult task of undertaking pipeline cooperation between India and Pakistan more feasible in the long term.

Socio-economic and environmental safeguards

To overcome the strong opposition that is apparent among certain groups of South Asian citizenry to cross-border energy projects,[32] a group of independent experts should create detailed blueprints of projects that address the local concerns of disenfranchisement, livelihoods and exploitation. Ali[33] has argued that pipelines such as the TAPI can be planned to reduce the socio-economic grievances that are often exploited by insurgent and terrorist groups to attract recruits. To gain acceptability of energy projects among the disenfranchised in Baluchistan and the Northeast Indian states, and to reduce incentives for sabotage by insurgents in these areas, planning must include adequate socio-economic programs. These initiatives can include infrastructure development, local employment generation, investment in education and healthcare, resettlement and rehabilitation and a transparent benefit-sharing model.

To gain wider acceptability of hydroelectric projects among Nepali citizens, South Asian countries must ensure that proper environmental planning and an acceptable compensation mechanism are taken into account. To address the disproportionate environmental cost borne by Nepal, a "beneficiary pay" principle can be implemented. Under this mechanism, the downstream country that is benefitting from upstream activities will be compensated for the services rendered.

Acceptance of international standards: Energy projects will fail to emancipate South Asia's poor if chronic corruption among the region's bureaucracy is left unchecked. South Asian countries should consider implementing the Extractives Industry Transparency Initiative (EITI) Standards, which is a global standard to promote accountability in the management of natural resources. Implementing the EITI standards would ensure that multilateral projects in South Asia are transparent, legal and sustainable. In addition, South Asian countries should also consider referring to the principles of the International Energy Charter (IEC). These international standards will give some reassurance to citizens of developing countries that the resources of their countries will not be syphoned off by corrupt government officials or MNCs. In addition, the IEC will give citizens a place to lodge their complaints. It is, therefore, important for South Asian countries to consider the use of internationally accepted standards and legislations to ensure transparency and accountability in energy projects.

Conclusion

Given that certain conditions are met, the implementation of multilateral energy projects in South Asia can facilitate a shift in the regional perception of energy security from one of sovereign control to a focus on availability and access, environmental sustainability and regional integration. While this would require the reorientation of long-established political expediencies by South Asia's political leaders, international actors also bear some responsibility in terms of technical consultation, political mediation and financing. A collective effort by international institutions, non-regional countries, global powers, and domestic political leaders is required for overcoming the challenges to multilateral energy projects in South Asia.

End Notes

1. *Statistical Review of World Energy* (London: BP, 2018).
2. Dadwal, Shebonti Ray. "Can the South Asian Gas Pipeline Dilemma be Resolved through a Legal Regime?" *Strategic Analysis* 35(5) (2011): 757–769.
3. Ebinger, Charles K. *Energy and Security in South Asia: Cooperation or Conflict?* (Washington, D.C: Brookings Institution Press, 2011).
4. Gippner, Olivia. *Energy Cooperation in South Asia: Prospects and Challenges* (Kathmandu, Nepal: South Asia Watch on Trade, Economics and Environment (SAWTEE), 2010).

5. Rasel, Aminur Rahman. "Now Joint Venture Coal Power Plant in India–Bangladesh." Dhaka Tribune (2016).

6. Karim, Rezaul. "Bangladesh Eyes 2,000 MW More from India by 2018". *The Daily Star* (2015).

7. IDSA. *Water Security for India: The External Dynamics*, IDSA Task Force Report (New Delhi: Institute for Defence Studies and Analyses, 2010).

8. Obaidullah, ANM. *Regional Hydropower Plants Legal Opportunities in Bhutan and Nepal* (Islamabad, Pakistan: The SAARC Energy Centre, 2010a).

9. Baruah, Amit. "India, Bhutan Update Friendship Treaty." *The Hindu* (2007).

10. Obaidullah, ANM. *Regional Hydropower Plants Legal Opportunities in Bhutan and Nepal* (Islamabad, Pakistan: The SAARC Energy Centre, 2010a).

11. IDSA. *Water Security for India: The External Dynamics*, IDSA Task Force Report (New Delhi: Institute for Defence Studies and Analyses, 2010).

12. SANDRP. *Bhutan Hydropower Developments in 2015* (Delhi: South Asia Network on Dams, Rivers and People, 2016).

13. Obaidullah, ANM. *Integrated Energy Potential of South Asia : Vision 2020* (Islamabad, Pakistan: The SAARC Energy Centre, 2010b).

14. Aminjonov, Farkhod. *Afghanistan's Energy Security: Tracing Central Asian Countries' Contribution* (Kabul, Afghanistan: Friedrich-Ebert-Stiftung, 2016).

15. Fareed, Madiha. "Prospects Brighten for Iran–Pakistan Gas Pipeline Project as Sanctions Lifted from Iran." *Dunya News* (2016).

16. ADB. "Turkmenistan, Afghanistan, Pakistan and India Establish Landmark TAPI Pipeline Company" (2014). http://www.adb.org/news/turkmenistan-afghanistan-pakistan-and-india-establish-landmark-tapi-pipeline-company, accessed January 1, 2016.

17. Huda, Mirza Sadaqat. "Regional Cooperation on Energy Security in South Asia: A Contemporary View". *SANDEE Newsletter* No. 29 (Summer 2015).

18. *Ibid.*

19. Asian Development Bank. "Power Interconnection Project to Strengthen Power Trade Between Afghanistan, Turkmenistan, Pakistan." News Release (2018). www.adb.org.

20. Bhonsale, Mihir. "Bhutan: Hydropower Cooperation under BBIN." *South Asia Weekly* (IX) (2016).

21. D'Souza, Shanthie Mariet. *The TAPI Pipeline: A Recipe for Peace or Instability?* (Institute of South Asian Studies, National University of Singapore, 2011).

22. Khan, Tawhidul Anwar. *Trans-boundary water issues in South Asia* (Dhaka: Bangladesh Environmental Lawyers Association (BELA), 2007).

23. ORF, IEF. "Regional Energy Cooperation: Accessing and Developing Hydrocarbon Resources in South Asia', ORF Seminar Series (1; New Delhi, India: India Energy Forum and The Observer Research Foundation, 2013).

24. Dadwal, Shebonti Ray. "Can the South Asian Gas Pipeline Dilemma be Resolved through a Legal Regime?" *Strategic Analysis* 35(5) (2011): 757–769.

25. Pande, Savita. "'Developing Energy Corridor from Central and West Asia to South Asia." *Towards an Asian Century: Future of Economic Cooperation in SAARC Countries* (Islamabad, Pakistan: Islamabad Policy Research Institute, 2013).

26. *Ibid.*

27. Dadwal, Shebonti Ray. "Can the South Asian Gas Pipeline Dilemma be Resolved through a Legal Regime?" *Strategic Analysis* 35(5) (2011): 757–769.

28. Hossain, Delowar. *Boundaries Undermined: The Ruins of Progress on the Bangladesh–India Border* (London: C Hurst and Co, 2013).

29. Bangladesh Enterprise Institute and Saferworld. *Safety and Security in South-East Border Area of Bangladesh* (Dhaka: Saferworld, 2013).

30. Khanna, Parag. *How to Run the World* (New York: Random House, 2011).

31. Ebinger, Charles K. *Energy and Security in South Asia: Cooperation or Conflict?* (Washington, D.C: Brookings Institution Press, 2011), p. 180.

32. Domestic opposition exists towards cooperation with India on energy projects in both Bangladesh and India. See Dipak Gyawali. Hype and Hydro in Nepal: What Went Wrong and What Corrective Measures are Needed? In Tomislav Delinic, Nishchal Pandey (Eds.). *Nepal's National Interests*, Centre for South Asian Studies, Kathmandu (2011); and Mirza Sadaqat Huda. Envisioning The Future of Cooperation on Common Rivers in South Asia: A Cooperative Security Approach by Bangladesh and India to the Tipaimukh Dam. *Water International* 42(1) (2017): 54–72.

33. Saleem, Ali. "Energizing Peace: The Role of Pipelines in Regional Cooperation". Brookings Doha Center Analysis Paper Number 2. (Doha, Qatar: Brookings Institution, 2010).

34. Zeshan, Muhammad and Ahmed, Vaqar. "Energy, environment and growth nexus in South Asia." *Environment, Development and Sustainability* 15(6) (2013): 1465–1475.

Chapter 4

Regional Integration through Energy Connectivity: The Low Hanging Fruit for South Asia[1]

Syed Munir Khasru

Introduction

The once blessed subcontinental land with seamless trade network along the Silk Road, South Asia now struggles to sustain its booming economic growth at the expense of its ever-increasing population. Lack of mutual trust, and resulting territorial disputes results in poor regional synergy and non-cooperative tendencies. Energy connectivity and trading in South Asia can be the game changer in ushering in an era of regional cooperation and prosperity. Noticeable traction has been achieved recently in energy cooperation through cross-border power trading and the momentum can be capitalised towards forging greater integration among the states. Synchronised policy framework, effective trading mechanism and

---

[1]This paper is an adaptation of the keynote address delivered at the ESI-ISAS workshop on "South Asia's Challenges and Opportunities in Sustainable Energy Transitions", held on 27 November 2017. The workshop was organised by the Energy Security Institute (ESI) of the National University of Singapore (NUS), in partnership with the Institute of South Asian Studies (ISAS), also from NUS.

efficient institutional delivery can help remove infrastructural and regulatory bottlenecks of energy cooperation that can catalyse socio-economic development for the 1.8 billion people in South Asia.

South Asia and the Low Integration

At 7.06% GDP growth rate, South Asia (SA) is now the fastest-growing region in the world. Expanding trade network coupled with favourable oil prices, is expected to boost economic growth from 7% in 2015 to 7.6% by 2017. It houses almost one-fourth of the world's population and has one of the oldest regional blocs in the neighbouring world. However, in terms of regional trade, SA is one of the least integrated regions in the world. Intra-regional trade in SA accounts for only 5% of the total trade, compared to 35% in East Asia, and 60% in the EU. Investment in the intra-regional trade is smaller than 1% of overall investment. To realise a harmonised regional integration, SA needs to exploit the full potential of trading and connectivity parameters. This is often hampered by the absence of adequate infrastructure and limited trade facilitation by regional platforms such as the Bay of Bengal Initiative for Multi-Sectoral Technical and Economic Cooperation (BIMSTEC), and South Asian Association for Regional Cooperation (SAARC).

Due to limited transport connectivity, outdated logistics and regulatory frameworks, and lack of trust, it costs more to trade within SA than countries outside of the region. In fact, it is 20% cheaper for India to trade with Brazil than with its neighbour Pakistan. If the bureaucratic hurdles and infrastructural barriers are removed, SA can experience increased intra-regional trade in goods from the current US$23 billion to more than double to US$50 billion. Some of the major factors that are deterring regional connectivity are briefly summarised as follows:

SAFTA and Non-Trade Barriers (NTB): Complex non-tariff barriers (NTBs) to trade are one of the main obstacles to regional trading in SA. There are three types of NTBs in the region, two of which are imposed at the borders during export and import. The NTBs include export subsidies, quotas and prohibitions on the export side; while import licensing, bans, and custom procedures are imposed on import. Finally, legal implications, i.e., quality specifications, product standards, environmental and labour standards impede the free flow of trade. Most of the NTBs in SA consist of technical barriers to trade and sanitary measures. These constraints made up 86.3% of all NTBs.

Inefficient Customs Procedure and Complex Rules of Origin: Limited resources of border logistics, poor connectivity and ineffective cross-border arrangements are some of the obstacles to SA intra-regional trade. When exporting a standardised container cargo, it takes 27 days to complete the trading formalities in SA. This time is spent to move goods from the manufacturers to seaports, excluding the paperwork for international shipments. It takes relatively more time on document preparation and ports clearance, but less time on inland transportation and cargo handling. In Bangladesh, a single export takes 25 days to complete, of which 17 days are spent on document preparation and customs clearance. Rules of origin are essential to trade local content with foreign partners, who require to claim the benefit of preferential tariffs within an economic zone or trade bloc. Compared to other trade platforms, South Asian Free Trade Association (SAFTA) has a complex and cumbersome structure for determining the rules of origin, making trade difficult.

Trans Loading Delay and Outdated Check Post: Adjacent trading borders in South Asian Countries (SAC) are mostly investor unfriendly — offering poor warehousing facilities. Parking spaces and transshipment yards are extremely limited in proportion to the number of cargo trucks. This delays the loading and unloading periods and extends the lead time. Most of the borders have limited testing laboratories and cold storage facilities and manual operations at the security gates take longer time as automated scanning systems are not available. The inspection and check booths at the SA borders create layers of inspection. There also is lack of initiatives in the area of creating a single window for export and import procedures, known as SWIFT (Single Window Interface for Facilitating Trade).

Lack of Harmony in Clearance Protocol and Transit Agreement: It takes a significant amount of time for border clearance for SA cross-border trading. This arises from asymmetric standards and clearance protocols among the border agencies. SA does not have any intra-country transit agreements. As a result, goods containers cannot produce bond at

travels across the region. This hampers the shipment procedure by imposing unnecessary restrictions or duty payments.

Lack of Port Infrastructure, Regulations and Dwell Time: SA does not
have efficient sea-ports facilities which makes it expensive and slow for
the shipping containers to enter or exit the ports. While SA has reduced
the gap with East Asia, some ports in India and Bangladesh take more
than three times longer to turn around a container ship than the world's
most competitive ports — Hong Kong, Shanghai and Singapore. The
region is still a minor player in global container port traffic, with a market
share that grew from 2.1% in 2000 to 2.9% in 2013. After 10 years of
average annual growth of 6%, the SAC desperately need to develop modern ports if it is to become an important player in the global trade.

Low Performance in the Global Value Chain (GVC): SA had only 10%
intra-regional participation in the Global Value Chain (GVC) in 2011,
whereas neighbouring Southeast Asia had the highest average share of 58%.
The poor GVC integration in SA comes from low levels of intra-regional
trade in intermediate goods and less dependent on neighbouring countries.
This region has substandard infrastructure quality that hampers the potential of regional integration — domestically, regionally and internationally.

No Negotiation on Services, Investment or Finance: Negotiation under
SAFTA has been limited to removing trade barriers for tangible non-
sensitive goods. No momentum has been reached on creating a framework
on trade in services, or intra-regional investment into infrastructural projects or finance.

Low Labour Mobility, Travel and Communication: International migration is increasing in the Asia-Pacific region, but labour markets remain
minimally integrated in SA due to the lack of infrastructural framework,
adequate regulatory mechanisms, political unwillingness and increased
security concern. Only 7% international calls made within SA compared to
71% in East Asia demonstrates the lack of people to people connectivity.

Historical Tension, Trust Deficit: Historical distrust in the region,
particularly the continued rivalry and enmity between the two largest

countries of the region, India and Pakistan, have cast a shadow over regional cooperation in SA. There have also been intermittent intra country tensions and hostility, India-Sri Lanka, Bangladesh–Pakistan, India–Nepal, which has not helped build trust and confidence in the region. As cooperation remains elusive, the region continues to suffer from technological backwardness, mass poverty, poor literacy rate, ill health, territorial disputes.

Energy Overview in South Asia

There is a wide variation in commercial energy resource allocation, and energy supply and demand in the SA. Energy consumption is only 707 kWh as opposed to the world average of 3,680 kWh with a growing energy demand of 4.6% per annum. Average electrification rate is 80%, whereas the neighbouring East Asia has 97%. While India, Pakistan and Bangladesh account for the major coal and natural gas resources, Bhutan and Nepal have large hydropower potential. However, hydrocarbon-based energy resources (coal and gas) are rapidly depleting. Most of the countries have vast renewable energy potential and sharing of these resources can lead to more optimal solutions of energy supply.

The key issues required to develop the SA energy sector are as follows:

- A regional power exchange market;
- Energy supply availability;
- Energy trade infrastructure; and
- Synchronised legal and regulatory frameworks.

However, the factors of low integration are hampering the cross-border energy trading in SA. Some of the long-standing factors restraining the SA energy connectivity are as follows:

- Complex trade mechanisms and investment restrictions;
- Relative difference in geographic size of the countries;
- Lack of appropriate policy framework on trade and investment mechanisms;
- Border conflicts and heightened security concerns;

- Limited connectivity, infrastructure, logistics and regulatory obstacles; and
- Sceptical mindset towards regional cooperation due to historical conflict and distrust;

Energy Cooperation: The Unexplored Potential

Regional energy trading in SA has been proven practically more viable due to its diverse resource allocation in both conventional and renewable energy. While other forms of connectivity, i.e., trade, transport and digital require long-term resource and regulatory planning, energy cooperation can be realised rather quickly by tapping into the unexplored trading potential as SA has massive unutilised potential of energy cooperation within its states. Most of its unexplored energy potential lies in renewables, such as hydropower, solar and wind power. Bhutan and Nepal are rich with hydropower resources that can be traded with immediate neighbouring countries. The Indian Ocean Region (IOR) countries have vast potential in wind and solar power. The coastal areas of IOR can generate wind power and fallow lands at the coastal areas have the potential to produce abundant solar power. Some of the unexplored energy potential in the region are summarised as in Figure 1.

Nepal's hydropower potential is 42 GW (technically and financially viable), even under the most conservative estimate. At present, only 800 MW is being exploited. Nepal and Bhutan generate 40 GW of hydroelectricity which can be exported to other member nations through common grid stations. Hydro potential includes Bhutan, Nepal, Pakistan and India: 30, 42, 59 and 150 GW, respectively. Wind Potential is total 183.74

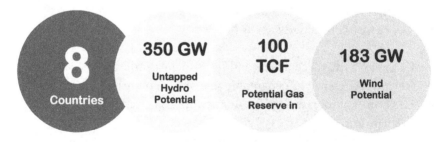

Figure 1:   The unexplored energy potential in SA.

GW from India, Nepal, Bhutan, Pakistan, Sri Lanka and Bangladesh. A conservative estimate of potential gas reserve in the Bay of Bengal is 100 trillion cubic feet.

Exploring the Gap in Energy Trading and Potentials of Renewable Energy

SA is highly dependent on imported crude oil and petroleum products for transport and commercial purpose. For example, Bhutan and Maldives meet 25% and 100% of their energy consumption, respectively, through import. Countries like Sri Lanka and Maldives, that lack fossil fuel sources, are heavily dependent on energy import. Even countries like India, Pakistan and Bangladesh also meet less of their domestic demand with local sources and confront rising energy import bills. India has the largest oil resource potential of 5,576 mtoe followed by Pakistan (3,600 mtoe) and Bangladesh (0.96 mtoe). Afghanistan, Bangladesh, India and Pakistan have natural gas reserves ranging from 120 bcm in Afghanistan to 7,985 bcm in Pakistan. Coal potential in India stands at 245,690 million tons, Pakistan 185,000 million tons, and Bangladesh 2,715 million tons. Coal is one of the largest fuel resources available in the region and has been mostly developed and utilised by India.

Biomass, wind, hydro and solar are available in many SA countries. Compared to traditional fossil–fuel-based sources, renewable technologies are still expensive. India has made strides in the renewables sector and is becoming one of the world's example of renewable energy revolution. Bangladesh too has forged ahead with renewables and today has the highest solar home penetration rate in the world. Other countries in the region have also started venturing into renewables, which can become more effective if concentrated regional effort is put into developing the market and investment climate for renewables. However, the region as a whole has poor share in renewable energy representing less than 5% of the total energy consumption.

The SA countries, particularly parts of Bangladesh, Sri Lanka and Maldives are extremely vulnerable to rising sea level due to climate change. To become energy secured and to reverse the effects of climate change, developing renewables in the region should be one of its foremost priorities. Hydropower potential in Nepal, wind potential in Afghanistan, and solar potential in India, Pakistan and Bangladesh can rightly help the region in meeting its energy demands without straining the environment. SA, as a unified singular block, can create the appropriate framework for renewables on a regional scale for attracting investment from large lenders into their exhausting energy sources.

South Asia: Country Specific Energy Scenario in a Nutshell

Every SA country has a unique situation, such as, gap in energy supply and demand, or insufficiency in the domestic market, or even the dominance of single fuel economy.

Afghanistan	**Afghanistan's** national energy consumption increased from 223,970 toe in 2002 to 340,311 toe in 2009. However, the country has the least electricity coverage with acute shortage of electricity coverage in dry seasons. Recently, this country has been connected to the CASA-1,000 network to export hydro electricity from the Central Asian countries.
Bangladesh	**Bangladesh** is heavily dependent on natural gas (62%). The existing resource is rapidly depleting as the country will have to actively look for alternative energy source for primary energy consumption after 2035. At present, almost 65% of the country has been brought under electrification. Apart from gas and limited coal reserves, Bangladesh has harnessed solar potential and has implemented solar PV applications especially in rural areas. Due to increased electricity usage in the ready-made garments (RMG) sector, Bangladesh is expected to face shortage in peak and base-load generation in the future.
Bhutan	**Bhutan** is the only country which is a net exporter of surplus hydro power in SA. At present, the country exports hydropower to India and is projected to have almost 30,000 MW of potential (23,760 MW economically feasible) hydro reserves.

(Continued)

(Continued)

India	Coal is the primary energy source in **India**. The country has around 75% of electricity coverage and currently trades power with Bangladesh, Bhutan and Nepal. In 2016, India declared the year with no power deficit and had a surplus of 3.1% during peak hours and 1.1% during the non-peak hours.
Maldives	**Maldives** generates only 300 MW from hydropower and imports 1,000 MW. Current demand is 2,000 MW and will be 3,000 MW by 2020. For most of its energy consumption, the country is almost entirely dependent on imported petroleum-based fuels sources. It has enormous potential of wind energy.
Nepal	**Nepal's** current electricity demand is 1,400 MW but has the generation potential of around 850 MW during the peak season. 75% of its produced energy comes from hydropower in Nepal. Like Bhutan, Nepal has abundant reserves (42 GW) in hydropower. However, the total hydropower energy in Nepal is expected to be fully exploitable within 5 years.
Pakistan	**Pakistan** has moderate reserve of gas, coal and nuclear as the primary energy sources. In addition, it has 3,600 mtoe of oil, 185,000 million tons of coal and 7,985 bcm of gas reserves. It has an average shortfall of 4 GW and 2 bcf per day. Like Afghanistan, Pakistan recently joined the CASA-1000 network to trade hydropower from Kyrgyzstan and Tajikistan.
Sri Lanka	With 85% uniform electricity reach, **Sri Lanka** has the highest electricity access in SA. The country is heavily dependent on oil import and has large trading potential with India. Due to increased dependence or import, Sri Lanka is projected to experience shortages in peak-load production with excess base-load generation.

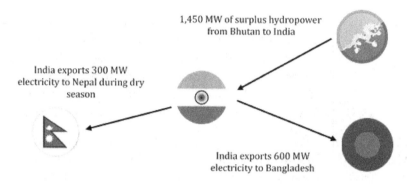

Figure 2:   Bilateral energy trading in SA.

Existing Power Trading Agreements

Limited bilateral power trade takes place between India and its three other neighbours: Nepal, Bhutan and Bangladesh (Figure 2).

- Electricity trading takes place between India–Bangladesh; Bhutan–India and India–Nepal.
- Petroleum products trading takes place between India–Bangladesh; Bhutan–Sri Lanka and Nepal–Sri Lanka (via the NE regions of India).
- Energy trading takes place both in forms of government-to-government (G2G) and commercial basis.

Potential of Energy Cooperation in South Asia

Considering the enormous potential in renewable energy, particularly in the hydropower, SA can harness the energy trading potential within the neighbourhood. Located at the centre of the SA, India can be the hub of energy cooperation. Except Maldives, most of the countries in the region can be integrated into the energy hub if it can develop a robust transmission system, Maldives too can join the network (Figure 3).

- **Afghanistan–Pakistan:** Through the Turkmenistan–Afghanistan–Pakistan–India (TAPI) Gas Pipeline, both Afghanistan and Pakistan can benefit from the energy-rich central Asia. Recently, the countries

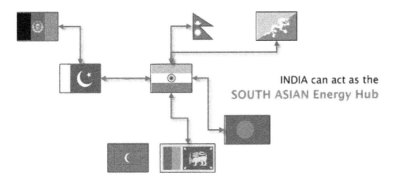

Figure 3: Energy cooperation through India.

have joined the CASA-1000 network and can act as the conduit of energy cooperation between Central Asia and SA and tap into the excess gas reserve from Kazakhstan and Turkmenistan.

- **Bhutan, Nepal–Bangladesh:** Being upstream countries with excess hydropower potential, Bhutan and Nepal can export the surplus energy to Bangladesh via India or directly to Bangladesh, provided that, the countries have built a high-voltage, direct current (HVDC) transmission network and synchronised grid interconnection.
- **Bhutan, Nepal–India:** Bhutan and Nepal can export their hydropower to India, especially in the energy starved northeast portions of the country.
- **India–Bangladesh:** The neighbouring countries can trade coal and hydro power. India can export its coal reserve via land ports or river channels. Bangladesh has the potential to export natural gas and refined bitumen to the northeastern part of India. In addition, India can secondarily export the hydro reserve from Bhutan to Bangladesh.
- **India–Pakistan:** India can collaborate into the Iran–Pakistan (IP) Pipeline and tap into the natural gas potential from Iran.
- **India–Sri Lanka:** The proposed India–Sri Lanka HVDC Grid Interconnection will be able to serve the need for regional grid connectivity. In addition, India has the potential of setting up an LNG terminal in suburban Colombo and solar power plant in the coastal areas of Sri Lanka.

Recent Developments in Energy Cooperation

- **Transmission Interconnection through SAARC Market for Electricity (SAME):** In 2014, SAARC Framework Agreement for Energy Cooperation (electricity) was signed to provide non-discriminatory access to the member states of SAARC. This framework has enabled exemption of export–import and custom duties for cross-border energy trading and provision of electricity exchange between buying and selling entities. In 2016, India released guidelines for the cross-border electricity trade, with the aim of introducing "greater transparency, consistency, and predictability in regulatory approaches" in SA. This agreement was forwarded as a crucial step to establish a SAARC Market for Electricity (SAME) on a regional basis. Adoption of the SAME agreement paved ways for developing a regional electricity market that inspired the BBIN network to integrate further with the ASEAN countries. India has recently acquired the "net exporter" status in SA and started selling electricity to Myanmar that opened up corridors to Thailand and the rest of Southeast Asia.

- **Increased Power Trading among Bangladesh–Bhutan–India–Nepal:** Currently, Bhutan is exporting 5,000–5,500 million units (MUs) of energy to India and Nepal is importing 190 MW of hydropower from India through 12 cross-border lines from Bihar. Bangladesh is importing 600 MW of electricity from India through two interconnections from Bengal and Tripura. From the increased cross-border wheeling capacity, export to Nepal and Bangladesh has increased to 250–280% in the last 3 years.

Although at a nascent stage, Bangladesh and India are laying several plans on:

- Doubling interconnection capacity from the existing 500 MW at the Baharmapur–Bheramara line;
- Increasing the capacity of Tripura–Comilla line to 200 MW;
- Laying a third interconnectivity from Assam's Bongaigaon to Bihar through Bangladesh; and
- Establishing a high-voltage, direct current (HVDC) line with capacity of 2,000 MW.

Deterrents of Energy Cooperation

Although SA has limited bilateral and trilateral energy cooperation due to the geographical proximity, several deterrents are hampering the potential of cross-country and multi-country energy cooperation. The deterrent factors can be primarily divided into: (1) Technical, (2) Political, and (3) Institutional constraints.

Technical constraints

- **Lack of Energy Sector Infrastructure:** Energy sector infrastructure is required in the form of electricity transmission lines, natural gas pipelines and crude oil and petroleum product pipelines. As of 2010, in the region only India has LNG terminals, but India does not have a well-developed natural gas pipeline network. This has hampered the development of a natural gas market in the country, since the demand and supply centres are not adequately connected. Bangladesh is also developing an LNG terminal at Maheshkhali (Southern part of the country), which will be the first fully integrated turnkey floating LNG terminal in the world. Many feasible hydropower projects are located in remote and mountainous areas of the Himalayas, where infrastructure, such as accessible roads and high-voltage transmission lines do not exist. This necessitates the development of this type of infrastructure for hydropower projects.
- **Lack of Standardised and Harmonised National Grid:** SA does not have any symmetric grid codes, operating procedures and standards to facilitate/promote cross-border electricity trade. As a result, the countries cannot channelize excess power to the neighbouring countries. Sri Lanka currently does not have any transmission lines. The recently planned 285-km undersea power transmission line between India and Sri Lanka is estimated to be completed at US$450 million (Figure 4).

Political barriers

- In the comparative geopolitical landscape, SA is a relatively unstable region. Through joint economic cooperation, SA has the potential to realise benefits of energy connectivity, trade and investment. However,

Figure 4:   The 360° impact due to low energy connectivity.

due to political distrust, ethnic conflicts and religious tensions, in many instances power and energy have come to be categorised as "sensitive" products for trade and regional exchanges resulting in inadequate cooperation among the member countries. This also has been a major factor why SA has failed to tap the potential of energy cooperation in most of the parts. The divisive political landscape of SAC deters the relevant political parties to adopt a synergistic energy cooperation strategy. In terms of investment, the energy projects require long-term pragmatic vision and political commitment regardless of change in regimes, something so far the SA leadership has not been able to deliver to its citizenry in the region.

Institutional constraints

- **Lack of Adequate Funding for Long-term Projects:** Investment prioritisation is equally important for energy cooperation. Most of the countries looking for investment in the energy sector opt for short-term or long-term projects, depending on the nature of the energy technology or indigenous energy consumption. However, regional energy platforms require investment in the long-term projects. As the multidimensional projects require transmitting energy through the member countries, there can be several factors associated with the regulatory and infrastructural network of the projects. As SA lacks synergistic regulatory platform, most of the private investors, entrepreneurs and development organisations hesitate to invest in the long-term projects.

- **Lack of Intercountry Coherent Policy Framework:** Energy markets in the individual countries are governed by individual legal, regulatory and policy frameworks, which differ from country to country. In some countries, energy falls under the purview of a single ministry. In others, there are multiple ministries handling energy-related and energy subsector issues. These differences add complexity to regional energy trade as it is difficult to draw one-to-one relationships across member states. Differences also exist in the structure and mandate of the regulators. Their roles range from multi-sector and overall energy sector to energy subsector regulations. India and Pakistan have separate sector regulators, while Bangladesh has one energy regulator. In the case of Sri Lanka, there is a Public Utilities Commission, which is not restricted to only the energy sector. Such divergence in the mandate of regulators across the region can impede the development of energy trade.

- **Lack of Financing for Renewables:** Although SA houses some of the major RE power potentials in the world, lack of investment outlook deters the process of harnessing the trade potential. The upstream countries, i.e., Nepal and Bhutan are still assessing the demand and supply condition in lieu to the actual potentials. These barriers of demand and supply side management and framework constraints can pose substantial burden and barriers for finance in the renewable energy sector. In addition, the technological differences within the member states require meeting several risk management considerations that may need significant change in the national RE policies.

Geopolitics of Energy Trade: The Game Changers

Energy can be a game changer for a specific country, or a region. Globally, there are many instances whereby energy has been a harbinger of peace and regional stability through inspiring cooperation among states who have not necessarily been political allies but have been wise enough to keep business and politics separate.

Western Europe and Russia

- The European natural gas sharing platform helped reducing territorial dispute by constructing pipelines between Western Europe and Russia in the 1980s at the height of the Cold War.
- The then Reagan administration in the US saw this as a threat to the balance of trade in Europe and vehemently opposed it.
- However, America's Western European allies went forward with the plan, refusing to back down to US pressures and sanctions.
- Today, Russia's oil and gas supplies represent a sizable portion of EU's total energy consumption.

Israel with Jordan and Turkey

- Relations between Israel and Turkey, one of the very few allies Israel has in the Muslim world, dissipated when Israeli troops stormed a Turkish humanitarian aid ship in 2010 to enforce a naval blockade in the Hamas-run Gaza strip, killing 10 Turkish activists.
- Israel recently discovered a huge reservoir of natural gas worth US$95 billion in Leviathan gas field in its shore under the Mediterranean Sea, far more than what it can consume, Israel moved to negotiate export deals and energy pipelines with its immediate Arab neighbours.
- Israel has already struck a US$10 billion export contract with Jordan, and is pushing forward similar combined exploration and pipeline deals with Turkey and Egypt. Israel has apologised and compensated Turkey for the 2010 attack on its aid ship.

Azerbaijan, Georgia and Turkey

- The 1,768 km long Baku–Tbilisi–Ceyhan long pipeline carries crude oil from the Azeri–Chirag–Guneshli oil field in the Caspian Sea to the Mediterranean Sea.
- The oil pipeline interconnects Baku (Azerbaijan), and Ceyhan, a port at the Mediterranean coast of Turkey, via Tbilisi (Georgia).
- Acts as a major regulator in the global oil politics. Through the oil pipeline, the South Caucasus has gained great strategic significance.
- Increased traffic of the international affairs from the US and other Western regions.
- The member states are trying to use the involvement to counterbalance the Russian and Iranian economic and military influence in the Caucasus region.

Russia and Japan

- Japan and Russia, two countries who are "technically" still at war, as no peace treaty has been signed between them after World War II due to territorial disputes over ownership of the four Kuril Islands.
- Russia has been occupying the islands since the war ended while Japan still claims ownership. The political leadership of both countries have shown wisdom and maturity in quarantining the geopolitical tensions, and not allowing it to interfere in matters where win–win economic gains can be reaped.
- Today Russia is a major exporter of crude oil to Japan, and there are ongoing talks to construct an undersea gas pipeline connecting Russia and Japan.

Policy Recommendations

Regional power market

Given the high opportunity cost of electricity shortages in the SA region, any effort to reduce those shortages will have significant economic benefits. An option available for the region to reduce electricity shortages is to promote enhanced electricity trade in any surplus that the SA country may have either daily or seasonally. Such enhanced electricity trade can be facilitated by a regional power exchange that would provide centralised control to increase opportunities for cross-border multilateral electricity trade among the SA countries, which are already interconnected or likely to have interconnections.

The following are recommended to develop a regional power market:

- Undertake a study of power system structures in the SAC, including the legal and regulatory aspects, and the power transmission system security and stability standards in the participating countries and their compatibility from a regional power trading perspective.
- A review of energy accounting systems, power generation scheduling, dispatch procedures and financial mechanisms for electricity transactions in the individual countries; detail the measures of harmonisation to allow feasible power trading; and analysis of regulatory, institutional and commercial requirements for cross-border energy trading.
- Development of a central structure for a regional power trade that can link the existing power exchanges platforms, with necessary operational modifications, with the extended power market for catering to the regional power trading market.

To enhance access to energy supply in the SA region:

- Expand the scope in Bhutan for further private sector participation in hydropower development and associated power transmission;
- Provide further targeted assistance to Nepal to strengthen its hydropower development framework in terms of detailed feasibility studies, financing mechanisms and formulation of public–private project implementation arrangements;
- Carry out further quantitative analysis to determine the attractiveness of SAC power purchase from large-scale high-efficiency centralised regional power plants, based on imported coal and natural gas from a LNG terminal;

- Review commercial risks associated with TAPI and IPI projects, particularly related to project cost, implementation and payment mechanisms, and compare with risks and costs associated with imported natural gas based on LNG.

Energy trade infrastructure

Poor investment in the cross-border energy trade in SA has largely been due to inadequate export oriented energy sector strategy development and unrealistic energy price expectations on the part of prospective energy receiving countries. Following policy initiatives are recommended to develop cross-border electricity trade infrastructure in the SA region:

- Identification of possible cross-border power transmission network and development of a regional power and energy database required to carry out power system studies capturing economic prices to the extent possible.
- Detailed examination of the interconnection modality, timing and operational feasibility.
- Technical and economic assessment of the interconnections, looking at the power system performance from a "with and without" interconnection perspective.
- Formulation of interconnector financing options through public sector; assessment of the level and modality of multilateral financing required to catalyse private sector investment.

Legal and regulatory framework

In terms of institutional improvements, energy markets in the individual states of SA are governed by respective legal, regulatory and policy frameworks. The following are recommended to facilitate harmonisation of the legal and regulatory framework:

- Synchronisation of regulatory and legal frameworks can be a strong incentive for both public and private sector investment. Such harmonisation can address: authorisation of electricity trading and unfettered access to power transmission, coordination of power system operation, inclusion of regional electricity trading in national energy policy, and developing mechanisms for regional dispute resolution.

- Inclusion of internationally recognised measures to the relevant policy framework to promote private sector participation and public–private partnership in cross-border power transmission and in renewables (hydro and thermal power) development.
- Promoting SA countries to be members of the Energy Charter Treaty (ECT) to provide greater security for cross-border energy trading related agreements and investments; ensuring security of supply to the energy consuming countries.

Risk mitigation strategy

- Bilateral agreements between governments;
- 'Risk Mitigating Principles' within the SAARC Framework Agreement for Energy Cooperation (electricity);
- SA countries follow similar technical standards in planning and operation following an archaic model. Therefore minimising technical risks; and
- Harmonisation of standards and codes related to cross-border trading.

The Energy Roadmap for Cooperation

Although SA has poor regional synergy, well planned and efficiently executed cooperation in the power and energy sector can promote regional integration and cooperation in other ancillary areas which include trade, infrastructure and connectivity. From the previous sections, the following summarises targeted initiatives as the primary important steps towards integration in the SA energy trading (Figure 5).

Capacity building and engagement

A platform for knowledge sharing and technical and instrumental training. This can be a hub of local counterparts, academic, policy makers and technical institutes. This platform can help engage the local counterparts, academics and technical institutes through:

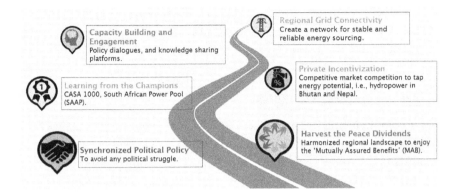

Figure 5: The roadblock for energy cooperation.

- Capacity building and training program;
- Knowledge sharing platforms.

Learning from the champions

Successful energy trading platforms can be the best source of adaptable energy trading models for setting policy and market mechanism. CASA-1000, and SAPP can be such ideal cases.

CASA-1000

- A hydropower sharing platform linking the Central Asia and SA power projects;
- Tajikistan and Kyrgyzstan will be able to export surplus hydroelectricity to Afghanistan and Pakistan during the summer, once the project completes in 2018;
- At the primary stage, Tajikistan and Kyrgyzstan will be able to export 1,300 MW of electricity to Afghanistan and Pakistan.

The South African Power Pool (SAPP)

- Formed in South Africa in 1995 and has proven to be successful in the long run;
- Provides electricity access to the rural communities;
- Improved relationships between the involved countries;
- Created strategies that support sustainable development priorities; and

- Member countries include: Angola, Botswana, Congo, Lethoso, Mozambique, Malawi, Namibia, South Africa, Swaziland, Tanzania, Zambia and Zimbabwe.

Synchronised political policy

For a complementary connectivity network in the power and energy sector, there is a need for an intra-governmental policy framework which is conducive for energy trade environment. This requires establishing of symmetric intra-government policies that supports plans, programs and projects for strengthening energy connectivity and trade in SA.

Regional grid connectivity

A regional grid network can provide a platform for stable and reliable energy interconnection. This will provide uninterrupted power to the grid and prevent seasonal blackouts and grid failures.

Private incentivisation

In addition to the setting up of a proper regulatory and technical framework, there is need for region-centric investment prioritisation that can provide incentives such as financial and technical assistance, grants and loans, i.e., for hydropower potential in Nepal and Bhutan electricity. This will encourage investment in regional energy projects.

Harvesting the peace dividend

In the conflict-prone and thorny political spectrum of SA, regional cooperation has remained elusive. By making the price of conflict high in a geopolitical context whereby the dividends of peace are even higher, good economics has the potential to neutralise destructive political rivalry and distrust in the region. Towards that end, energy cooperation, connectivity and trade can be the game changer in SA that otherwise continues to be one of the least integrated regions. A region which has much to lose by not cooperating in an energy starved population vying to climb up the ladder of economic growth and prosperity. Hence, in one of the most fragmented regions of the world, energy is the low hanging fruit which has something to offer to everybody and much to lose for someone choosing to be left out. To overcome the constraints and to unleash the benefits of energy cooperation, the doctrine of "Mutually Assured Benefits" (MAB) needs to be understood better and implemented with due diligence by the political leadership who has the ultimate responsibility to lead cooperation and integration in the region.

Conclusion

With a rich and diversified socio-economic background, South Asia has one of the largest unexplored energy mother lodes in the world. Rapid urbanisation and industrialisation are putting immense pressure on the existing energy infrastructure. To meet the soaring economic and regional development needs, energy connectivity and trade can be one of the best policy options to opt for in the region. Otherwise, SA will continue to be mired in decades of poor connectivity, insignificant regional trade, weak economic links, and little potential to achieve shared prosperity in a region which otherwise has a rich history of shared culture, values, heritage and people to people proximity.

End Notes

1. Asian Development Bank. *Energy Trade in South Asia: Opportunities And Challenges* (Manila: Asian Development Bank, 2011).
2. Dutta, S. *India Becomes Net Exporter of Power* (2017). Retrieved from Times of India: https://timesofindia.indiatimes.com/business/india-business/india-becomes-net-exporter-of-power/articleshow/57898582.cms.
3. Nataraj, G. *Break Down the Barriers to Trade in South Asia* (2014). Retrieved from East Asia Forum: http://www.eastasiaforum.org/2014/03/14/break-down-the-barriers-to-trade-in-south-asia/.
4. Rajiv Kumar, M. S. *India's Role in South Asia Trade and Investment Integration* (Manila: Asian Development Bank, 2009).
5. Tasneem Mirza, E. B. *Addressing Hard and Soft Infrastructure Barriers to Trade in South Asia* (Manila: Asian Development Bank, 2013).

6. World Bank. *South Asia Economic Focus Spring 2015* (Washington DC: World Bank, 2015).
7. World Bank. *Competitiveness of South Asia's Container Power* (Washington, DC: World Bank, 2016).
8. World Bank. *Electric Power Consumption (kWh per capita)* (2016). Retrieved from World Bank: https://data.worldbank.org/indicator/EG.USE.ELEC.KH.PC.
9. World Bank. *The Potential of Intra-regional Trade for South Asia* (2016). Retrieved from World Bank: http://www.worldbank.org/en/news/infographic/2016/05/24/the-potential-of-intra-regional-trade-for-south-asia.
10. Connecting to Value Chains: The Role of Trade Costs and Trade Facilitation. In *OECD, Aid for Trade: At a Glance* (Paris: WTO, 2015), pp. 165–184.
11. *World Trade Statistical Review* (WTO, 2016).

Chapter 5

Progression of Renewable Energy Development for Electricity in South Asia: Drivers and Challenges

Thusita Sugathapala

Introduction

Although South Asia is one of the fastest growing regions in the world, their socio-economic profiles indicate the challenges of addressing the growing demands of their economies and population, particularly in the energy sector. Heavy dependence on imported fossil fuels, lack of energy security due to single major source of supply, fragile electricity supply infrastructure, excessive losses in transmission and distribution networks, and low level of electrification in general are some key issues. On the other hand, as the underpinning factor of the economy, each country has pledged to provide reliable, affordable and secure energy supply, while promoting environmental sustainability, as envisaged by the UN Sustainable Energy for All (SE4ALL) initiative, which requires a paradigm shift in the policies for energy sector. The key strategic approach in achieving this uphill task is the promotion of renewable energy (RE) resources, and all

South Asian countries have taken optimistic policy initiatives at the highest levels to facilitate technological innovation and creation of new markets and industries, with particular emphasis on RE for electricity. Despite tremendous technical potentials and benefits, the commercial exploitation of RE in South Asia faces challenges ranging across several areas including policy, institutional, financial, information and human resource, and technical aspects. There are innovative policy responses and programmes initiated by the governments to address some of these barriers, but more forward-looking policies and strategies are necessary to promote RE for electricity in South Asia, with emphasis on regional-level cooperation for knowledge-sharing and technology transfer.

Context

Globally, the energy sector development, particularly RE, has received much attention in the context of sustainable development, not only due to its central role in achieving inclusive socio-economic development but also due to its impact on the much-spoken topics of greenhouse gas (GHG) emission and climate change. The 2030 Agenda for Sustainable Development, the new global framework adopted by the UN General Assembly on 25 September 2015, has set a specific goal (SDG 7) on ensuring access to affordable, reliable, sustainable and modern energy for all, which highlights the need for increasing substantially the share of RE in the global energy mix by 2030,[1] which is inconsistent with the SE4ALL initiative's three interlinked objectives on energy access, energy efficiency (EE) and RE.[2] In particular, SE4ALL initiative calls action for doubling the share of RE in the global energy mix (i.e., 18% in 2010 to 36% in 2030, which is a revised target of 15% in 2009 to 30% in 2030 set during the 2012 Year of SE4ALL based on provisional data).[3]

Another driver for RE is linked to global climate change and its impacts. The fifth assessment report (AR5) of the Intergovernmental Panel on Climate Change (IPCC) concludes that despite the variety of existing policy efforts and the existence of the United Nations Framework Convention on Climate Change (UNFCCC) and the Kyoto Protocol, GHG emissions have grown at about twice the rate in the recent decade (2000–2010) than any other decade since 1970. The current trajectory of global annual and cumulative emissions of GHGs is inconsistent with the widely discussed goals of limiting global warming at 1.5–2°C above the pre-industrial level. As solutions, IPCC AR5 presents three categories of energy system-related mitigation measures: the de-carbonisation of the energy supply sector, final energy demand reductions and the switch to low-carbon energy carriers, including electricity, in the energy end-use sectors.[4] Consequently, 196 Parties in the UNFCCC adopted the Paris Agreement in 2015, a new legally binding framework for an internationally coordinated effort to tackle climate change, which aims to hold global temperatures well below 2°C above pre-industrial levels and to pursue efforts to limit the temperature increase to 1.5°C. Nationally determined contributions (NDCs), which are at the heart of the Paris Agreement, embody efforts by each country to reduce national emissions and adapt to the impacts of climate change. The energy sector components of the respective NDCs of all the South Asian countries include promotion of RE, with particular emphasis on electricity generation.[5]

The relevance of the global challenges and drivers highlighted above to the South Asian region is substantial, as it represents one-fourth of the world's population and as a significant section of the population does not have access to electricity or other forms of modern energy services. Further, increasing dependence on imported fossil fuels has adversely affected the economic development and energy security in general. These challenges are likely to get more complex as energy demand is growing to keep pace with an expanding population and economy.[6] A business-as-usual (BAU) scenario of primary energy is projected to increase by 210% from 2010 to 2035, while that of electricity generation is set to rise by 350%. South Asia's net imports of fossil fuels are projected to increase more than 300% during the same period.[7] Though South Asia possesses significant indigenous energy resources, they remain largely underdeveloped. Almost all countries in the region have set up agencies to popularise and commercialise RE technologies, thereby pursuing measures to diversify their traditional supply mix.[8]

As one of the key options to face the challenges in the energy sector in South Asia, promotion of RE, particularly for electricity generation, has received increasing interest in the recent past. This chapter analyses the progression of RE development for electricity in South Asia.

South Asian Region Outlook

South Asia, comprised of eight developing countries, namely Afghanistan, Bangladesh, Bhutan, India, Maldives, Nepal, Pakistan and Sri Lanka, is one of the most populous regions of the world, having about one-fourth of the world population but only about 1/30th of world's land area. The key socio-economic indicators for South Asian countries are presented in Table 1. In 2016, though the South Asia region's gross domestic product (GDP) per capita of US$1,638 was well below US$10,190 of the world, the annual growth rate of GDP per capita was 5.5%, which was significantly higher than that of other regions and the world average. South Asia is also a region of stark contrasts: country population varied from 0.417 million in Maldives to 1.324 billion in India; land area varied from 0.0003 million km² in Maldives to 2.97 million km² in India and population density (per km²) varied from 21 in Bhutan to 1,426 in Maldives. In 2016, the per capita GDP ranged from US$562 in Afghanistan to US$9,875 in the Maldives, while annual growth rate of GDP per capita varied from –0.7% in Nepal to 6.6% in Bhutan.[9] The Human Development Index (HDI) in 2015 varied from 0.479 in Afghanistan to 0.766 in Sri Lanka, with a South Asia regional average of 0.621.[10]

Table 1:   Key socio-economic indicators for South Asia.[11,12]

Country	Population in 2016 (million)	Population density in 2016 (per km²)	Urban population in 2016 (% of total)	GDP per capita in 2016 (US$)	GDP per capita growth (annual %)	HDI in 2015 (and world rank)
Afghanistan	34.7	53	27	561.8	–0.3	0.479 (169)
Bangladesh	163.0	1,252	35	1,358.8	6.0	0.579 (139)
Bhutan	0.8	21	39	2,773.5	6.6	0.607 (132)
India	1,324.2	445	33	1,709.6	5.9	0.624 (131)
Maldives	0.4	1,426	47	9.875.3	3.8	0.701 (105)
Nepal	29.0	202	19	729.1	–0.7	0.558 (144)
Pakistan	193.2	252	39	1,443.6	3.4	0.550 (157)
Sri Lanka	21.2	332	18	3,910.0	4.0	0.766 (73)
South Asia	1,766.4	370	33	1,637.9	5.5	0.621 (–)
World	7,442.1	57	54	10,189.6	1.3	0.717 (–)

In all the South Asian countries, the percentage of urban populations is less than 50% (ranging from 18% in Sri Lanka to 47% in
Maldives). Therefore, high migration of population to urban areas
could be expected in years to come, and together with high economic
growth rate, countries in South Asia would face an uphill task of progressing towards inclusive socio-economic development, particularly
achieving UN sustainable development goals (SDGs). As energy
underlies the economy, the energy sector is expected to play a central
role in the development agendas. Therefore, the South Asian region's
energy sector, particularly the power sector, is reviewed in the following
section in greater detail.

South Asian Region Power Sector

Overview

As with socio-economic indicators, energy sectors in South Asian countries represent wide diversity and differences. Table 2 presents some key
energy and environment indicators for South Asia.[13,14,15] In the year
2015, per capita energy consumption ranged from 90 kg of oil equivalent
(kgoe) in Afghanistan to 857 kgoe in Maldives. The South Asian average value of 510.2 kgoe (or 16.3 kWh/day) is much less than the world
average of 1,854.9 kgoe (or 59.1 kWh/day). The minimum primary
energy supply requirement for a country to reach developed status of
economy is considered to be in the range 50–100 kWh/capita/day (or
1,570–3,140 kgoe/capita/year).[16] Figure 1 presents the variation of HDI
with per capita primary energy supply across countries, which highlights
the strong coupling between energy and economy. Accordingly, the
energy sector has to play a leading role in socio-economic development.

Per capita electricity consumptions too reflect the wide variations,
from 49 kWh in Afghanistan to 2,420 kWh in Bhutan. Again, the
South Asian average value of 708 kWh is significantly lower than
the global average of 3,125 kWh. Though there has been higher
growth of electrification in all the countries in South Asia, still the
electrification rate varies considerably, from 43% in Afghanistan to
100% in Maldives.

Table 2:   Key energy and environment indicators for South Asian countries.[17-20]

Country	Per capita primary energy supply in 2015 (kgoe)	Per capita electricity consumption in 2014 (kWh)	Electrification rate in 2012 (% of total population)	Renewable electricity output in 2014 (% of total electricity output)	Per capita GHG emissions in 2014 (t CO_{2e})	Ecological footprint per capita in 2010 (gha)
Afghanistan	90.0	3	43.0	85.32	0.29	0.79
Bangladesh	208.8	310	59.6	1.32	0.44	0.72
Bhutan	355.0	2,420	75.6	99.99	1.26	0.79
India	565.6	806	78.7	15.42	1.67	1.16
Maldives	857.0	2,283	100.0	0.61	3.55	—
Nepal	341.1	139	76.3	99.97	0.28	0.98
Pakistan	487.3	471	93.6	30.22	0.80	0.79
Sri Lanka	477.9	535	88.7	39.22	0.88	1.32
South Asia	510.2	708	78.9	16.80	1.40	1.07
World	1,854.9	3,125	84.5	22.35	4.95	2.84

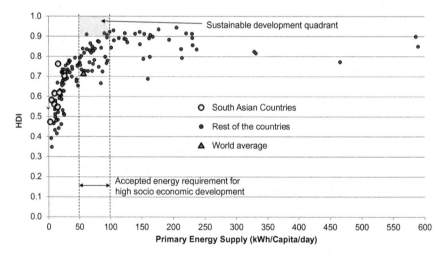

Figure 1:   HDI vs primary energy supply of countries in the world.[21]

Environment dimensions of economy and energy[22,23]

The main concern of the trends in socio-economic development in general, and energy sector in particular, is the impact on the ecosystems that sustains societies, which in turn creates economies. One key indicator of the impact of energy sector on environment is the GHG emissions from human activities, which is considered to be the most significant driver of the observed changes in the climate system since the mid-20th century.[24] As shown in Table 2, the per capita GHG emissions in South Asian countries are well below the world average, except for Maldives where the electricity generation is entirely based on oil, which could be attributed primarily to the lower per capita energy consumption and use of RE resources.

Another key indicator that reflects human impacts on ecosystem is the ecological footprint, which is a measure of human demand on nature. Table 1 provides the figures of the ecological footprint per capita in 2010 in global hectares (gha) for South Asian countries and the world average. One of the key elements of the ecological footprint is the carbon footprint, directly linked to the energy sector. As with HDI vs primary energy supply, a similar trend could be found in the variation of ecological footprint with another global development indicator namely UN inequality-adjusted human development index (IHDI), as illustrated in Figure 2.[25,26] The positions of South Asian countries reveal that the use of natural resources is well within the bio-capacity, demonstrating the environmental sustainability of the economies in the region. However, in general, the levels of human development are far from satisfactory and the situation with environmental

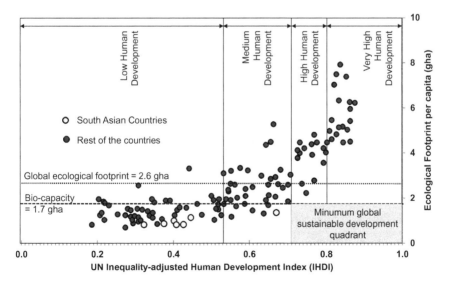

Figure 2: Ecological footprint vs IHDI of countries in the world.[27]

sustainability may change with increasing socio-economic development in coming years, particularly if the current economic development models continued to be followed.

Further, both Figures 1 and 2 signify that the development pathways of countries in South Asia towards the much anticipated sustainable development are more challenging than moving along the typical trends reflected by the positions of other countries at different stages of development. On the other hand, as all the countries in South Asia still use less energy and less natural resources (as reflected by per capita energy consumptions and ecological footprints), they have more opportunities to move away from the traditional development models and follow more sustainable pathways. Such efforts require fundamentally a transformational change in the economy, for instance, moving away from the linear economy model to a circular economy model where reliance on energy from renewable sources is a fundamental principle.[28] This inevitably demands for a related paradigm shift within the energy sector too, particularly the promotion of low-carbon technologies such as REs for electricity generation more aggressively. Accordingly, deeper insight into the role and potential of RE resources is required in gaining better understanding of the situation for planning and implementing futuristic programmes. The following section is devoted to a review of the RE development in the power sector in South Asian countries.

RE scenarios and the power sector

The South Asian region has huge technical potential for RE resources. Exploitation of these resources is limited by not only technical and financial factors, but also by environmental as well as social issues. Though some estimates on the resource potentials are available in the literature[29-33]; there are gaps in the information that hinder the establishment of a comprehensive database on RE resource potentials. Table 3 presents the RE resource potential for electricity generation in South Asian countries derived from the Global Energy Resources Database of Shell Global.[34] The electricity consumption in year 2014 is also presented for comparison. These estimates show that the present utilisation of the RE resources for electricity generation is about 0.9%.

As can be seen from Table 3, though there exists a tremendous resource potential within South Asia, use of REs for electricity generation

Table 3:   Estimates of RE resource potentials for electricity generation.[35]

| Country | Exploitable electricity generation potential (TWh/year) | | | | | | Renewable electricity output in 2014 (TWh) |
	Solar PV	Wind (on-shore & off-shore)	Biomass	Hydro	Geo-thermal	Total	
Afghanistan	2,014.7	56.7	3.9	8.9	75.0	2,159.2	1.43
Bangladesh	1,125.3	181.9	22.2	12.8	16.1	1,358.3	0.67
Bhutan	9.2	—	—	40.0	4.7	53.9	1.92
India	10,789.4	1,992.2	377.8	367.5	480.6	14,007.5	166.85
Maldives	3.9	1.7	—	—	—	5.6	0.01
Nepal	434.4	0.0	4.7	11.4	17.2	467.8	4.06
Pakistan	4,901.4	191.4	12.2	120.3	27.8	5,253.1	29.57
Sri Lanka	135.0	93.9	9.2	6.7	7.8	252.5	4.39
South Asia	19,413.3	2,517.8	430.0	567.5	629.2	23,557.8	208.90

is still very limited. Further, it only contributes to 16.8% of the electricity output in the region (see Table 2), which signifies the high dependence on fossil fuels particularly for electricity generation, except for Bhutan, Nepal and Afghanistan (see Table 2). This aspect is clarified more in Figure 3, which presents energy source mix in the power sector.[36] Another salient feature is the dependence on single major source of supply: hydro in Bhutan (99%), Nepal (93%) and Afghanistan (59%); natural gas in Bangladesh (76%); coal in India (60%) and Pakistan (68%); and oil in Maldives (100%). In Sri Lanka, large hydro together with new renewable sources (which include small hydro, wind, solar and biomass) contribute to about 50% of the total installed capacity, and the balance is accounted for by coal and oil. The future electricity generation expansion plan in Sri Lanka also has given more emphasis to fuel diversification and promotion of RE resources, limiting contribution of largest single source (coal) to less than one-third of the total installed capacity over the next 20 years. Still about half of the installed capacity would be from imported fossil fuels (coal, natural gas and oil).[37] These situations would challenge the energy security aspect of the power sector of South Asian countries.

The diversity across South Asian countries discussed earlier is again reflected in relation to the contribution of RE in the total electricity generation, covering the full range of almost 0% (in Maldives) to almost

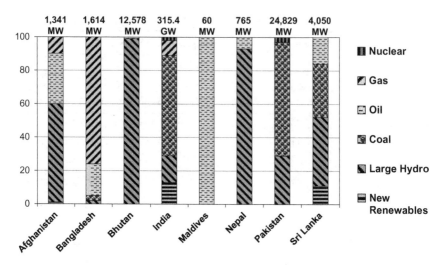

Figure 3:   Energy source mix in the power sector of South Asian countries.[38]

100% (in Bhutan and Nepal). The information in Figure 3 also illustrates that the primary contribution to renewable electricity is from large hydro (having about two-third of the installed capacity), and the new RE resources such as wind and solar are yet to be exploited at a large scale (except for India and Sri Lanka, where the new RE contributions are 13% and 11%, respectively). In this regard, proposals for development of new REs are highlighted in NDCs (or INDCs) submitted by all countries in South Asia (except in Maldives's NDCs), with emphasis on electricity generation as part of the energy sector mitigation options. Some of these interventions proposed have specific targets either as a percentage contribution or absolute values of installation capacity. Others are more qualitative, particularly highlighting government commitments for the promotion of RE as means of reducing GHG emissions with respect to the BAU scenario. A summary of power sector NDC targets related to REs is presented in Table 4.[39]

Another decisive factor that affects the development of RE in the power sector is the infrastructure such as electricity transmission lines, substations and access roads. In fact, building adequate capacity to evacuate power is fundamental for promoting and developing RE for large-scale power generation. All of the countries in South Asia lack the

Table 4: RE-related interventions proposed under NDCs of South Asian countries.[40]

Country	Interventions and targets proposed in NDCs
Afghanistan	• Target in all sectors: 13.6% reduction in GHG emissions by 2030. • Sectors related to energy: ○ Energy production (hydropower, solar power systems, wind and biomass). ○ Power plants: fuel shift to natural gas and renewables.
Bangladesh	• Target in all sectors: 20% reduction in GHG emissions by 2030 (5% unconditional and 15% conditional). • Mitigation actions/targets related to RE: ○ 400 MW of wind, 1000 MW of utility-scale solar. ○ Solar home systems as off-grid electricity access (ongoing action).
Bhutan	• Target in all sectors: Remain carbon neutral where emission of GHGs will not exceed carbon sequestration by the forests (of 6.3 million tons of CO_2). • Strategies, plans and actions related to RE: ○ Promote clean RE generation: Hydropower development with support from climate market mechanisms to reduce emissions within Bhutan and the region by exporting surplus electricity.
India	• Targets: ○ Reduce emissions intensity of GDP by 33–35% by 2030 from 2005 level. ○ To achieve about 40% cumulative electric power installed capacity from non-fossil fuel-based energy resources by 2030. • Priority areas related to RE: ○ Promote RE and increasing the share of alternative fuels in overall fuel mix. • Other specific targets/actions: ○ 60 GW of wind, 100 GW of solar and 10 GW of biomass by 2022. ○ Pursue development of hydro more aggressively.
Maldives	• Target in all sectors: 24% reduction in GHG emissions by 2030 (10% unconditional and 12% conditional). • Sectors related to energy: ○ Electricity production.
Nepal	• Target in power sector: 80% electrification through RE sources by 2050. • Other targets related to RE: ○ Under the National Rural and Renewable Energy Programme: 25 MW small hydro, 600,000 solar home systems, 1,500 institutional solar power systems. ○ Expand the energy mix focusing on renewables by 20% by 2020.

(Continued)

Table 4:   (*Continued*)

Country	Interventions and targets proposed in NDCs
Pakistan	• Target in all sectors: Reduce up to 20% of GHG emissions by 2030. • Mitigation Options in Energy Supply Sector related to RE: ○ Large scale and distributed grid-connected solar, wind and hydroelectricity.
Sri Lanka	• Target in all sectors: Reduce the GHG emissions by 20% in the energy sector (4% unconditional and 16% conditional) and by 10% in other sectors (3% unconditional and 7% conditional) by 2030. • Specific targets related to RE: ○ 514 MW of large-scale wind, 115 MW of solar, 105 MW of biomass, and 176 MW of mini-hydro by 2030. ○ Strengthen sustainable energy policies for increasing the share of RE from the existing 50% to 60% in 2020 (and maintain at the same level thereafter).

required power sector infrastructure to absorb RE, in addition to those required to serve the ever-increasing demand for energy services. In general, the national and regional electricity transmission grids are planned by considering the large-scale centralised thermal generation plants and main load centres, which undermines the future expansions of REs where the high resource potential sites could be in more remote and less accessible locations. Further, inherent variability of RE resources (in particular solar and wind) demand more advance power network infrastructure with state-of-the-art information and control technologies and power electronics, which could facilitate efficient coordination between demand and supply variations to optimise reliability and productivity of the overall power system. The development of such infrastructure will need to be technically viable, financially feasible and environmentally sustainable for mainstreaming electricity generation from RE sources.[41-43]

There are also other deficiencies in the South Asian power sector including fragile electricity supply infrastructure, resulting in electricity shortfalls and extensive electricity outages, and also the supply-side EE issues. In particular, significantly high losses in electricity transmission and distribution (T&D) networks in South Asia are frequently highlighted.[44] The cost competitiveness of RE would greatly be affected by the excessively high losses, particularly in cases where the RE plants are located far away from the demand centres. In 2014, the T&D losses were reported as 11.4% in Bangladesh, 19.42% in India, 32.21% in Nepal, 17.41% in Pakistan and 11.4% in Sri Lanka, and overall 18.94% in South Asia, all of which are two-digit numbers.[45] Thus, more emphasis should be given by the electricity utilities to reduce network losses to single-digit levels, which many developed countries achieved decades ago.

Drivers and Challenges For RE Development in the South Asian Region

Drivers

As highlighted in the section "Context", the interest of RE resources for electricity generation has emerged with global and local challenges, not only in the power sector but also in the much broader context of socio-economic development. Thus, the drivers for RE development originated from many sectors. Perhaps the most significant one is the central role of REs in making a transformational change in the power sector that is necessary for steering the nations towards much anticipated sustainable development, as shown in Figures 1 and 2. The conventional linear economy model (i.e., take–make–dispose) would not help out the nations to face daunting tasks in the energy sector in the years to come, and hence the concept of circular economy with a renewable resource-dominant energy sector is the key to success.[46] Thus, the need to achieve sustainability targets becomes a driver for RE developments. Under such an overarching perspective, multiple drivers for RE development would also emerge, as discussed below.

Another significant driver for exploitation of indigenous RE resources is the contribution to reduce the imported fossil fuel dependence, thereby mitigating its adverse impacts on national economy (drain of foreign reserves). Further, the contribution to the enhancement of energy security aspects through diversification of supply sources, together with the availability of RE resources on a sufficient scale, also becomes a key driver for the promotion of RE. Here, it becomes imperative to develop and implement an RE roadmap by selecting a combination of RE resources and technologies based on sustainability criteria covering technical, financial, environmental and social indicators.[47] As RE resources are diverse and distributed, harnessing them could contribute to other societal goals and national targets, such as those related to rural electrification and local socio-economic developments.

Development of RE technologies also provide provisions for local value addition, job creation and more business opportunities. These in turn provide more prospects for local R&D, inventions and innovations in the energy sector, thus providing openings not only for regional/international collaborations for capacity building and technology transfer but also for knowledge creation, sharing and application. Overall, development of the RE sector will have its imprint on wider cross-sections of the society and different sectors of the economy than just being limited to the energy sector. Thus, the presence of such multiple benefits too become a driver for RE.

The continuous technological development and cost reduction of energy conversion and storage systems have led to a much more favourable environment for large-scale adoption of REs. In addition to the progressions in typical areas such as energy conversion efficiencies, materials, manufacturing systems, and logistics, the potential for adoption of RE is further enhanced by advancements in weather forecasting, ICT and control protocols, distributed energy systems, hybrid energy systems, substation automation and grid storage technologies. In line with these, sharp reduction in capital costs of REs, particularly for solar photovoltaic (PV), onshore and offshore wind, was seen in the recent past. In 2016 alone, average capital cost of solar PV dropped by 13% to US$1,200/kW, while those for onshore and offshore wind dropped by 11.5% and 10% to US$1,600/kW and US$4,000/kW, respectively. Such cost reductions have been instrumental for accelerated growth in RE for electricity generation. For example, although the new RE contribution (except large hydro) to the total electricity generation is about 10%, in 2016, the RE capacity addition was 55% of all the generating capacity added globally, the highest proportion in any year to date.[48] Thus, maturing of niche RE technologies, technology innovations and weakening RE cost hypothesis represent a driver for RE sector developments.

As the use of depleting natural resources and adverse impacts on the environment during the development and implementation stages of RE projects are much lower than that of conventional energy systems, the environmental dimension of energy highly favours the development of RE. This is clearly evident from the dynamism of the RE sector throughout the world, in relation to the changes in policies, politics, governance, institutionalisations, strategies, action plans, R&D, innovations, technology transfer, finance mobilisation, education, etc., as a result of the severity of the climate change issue associated with GHG emission and global warming. For example, finance for RE sector continues to dominate over those related to conventional fossil fuel technologies. Investments in new RE capacity were roughly double that in fossil fuel generation in 2016 for the fifth successive year.[49] The role of RE in the mitigation of climate change is well recognised by the global community, with all the countries in South Asia too committed to support the global actions, as reflected in NDCs (see Table 4). These commitments will enhance the access to finance/clean funds, which could be effectively used in leapfrogging to an RE-dominant power sector. Thus, increasing access to finance and growing investment represent another key driver for progression in the RE sector.

Challenges

Though there are several drivers (and benefits) of increased use of RE for electricity generation as highlighted in the previous section, the power sector is still dominated by fossil fuels and contribution from RE is not very significant globally as well as regionally (see Table 2). This implies the presence of challenges (including barriers/risks) surpassing the drivers. The situational analysis presented in sections "South Asian Region Outlook" and "South Asian Region Power Sector" highlights, in general, areas where the sector development is affected, and section "Drivers" provides some insight into the gaps in South Asian region that affect the full exploitation of the conditions created by the drivers. In order to have a methodical approach while identifying and analysing, it is rational to categorise challenges under different facets, namely policy and governance, technical, financial and market, and capacity and information. Table 5 provides a summary of challenges to harness and commercialise RE resources and technologies, signifying the host of barriers and risks for RE sector development.

Table 5:   Challenges for the promotion of RE for electricity generation.[50,51]

Challenge	Interventions and targets proposed in NDCs
Policy and Governance	o Lack of cohesion in related policies. o Regular changes in policies and institutional arrangements. o Gaps between policy and actions (non-implementation of policies). o Lack of government priorities for RE, particularly at fund allocation stages. o Lack of coordination and interaction among institutions and stakeholders. o Weak environmental regulations. o Lack of technical standards and technology certification schemes. o High perceived risks and uncertainties.
Technical	o Lack of standardised RE technologies. o Inadequate and fragile electricity supply infrastructure. o Limited facilities to design, install, operate, manage and maintain modern RE systems. o Technological constraints for comprehensive resource monitoring and mapping. o Lack of dynamic modelling/advanced forecasting tools. o Limited local manufacturing of specialised equipment. o Insufficient or absence of technology certification/testing facilities.
Financial and Market	o Small economies of scale, high capital costs and long payback periods. o Lack of incentives for private sector involvement. o Lack of access to credit and insufficient government financial support. o Absence of or insufficient feed-in tariff structure. o Fossil fuel subsidies/distorted market.
Capacity and Information	o Lack of information about RE resources and technologies, demonstration projects of modern technologies, equipment suppliers and potential financiers. o Insufficient information on RE for policymaking and mobilising civil society. o Insufficient expertise in business management and entrepreneurial skills. o Lack of expertise and services in system design, installation and O&M. o Lack of long-term resource data. o Lack of R&D efforts.

Conclusions

All the countries in South Asia face daunting tasks in the energy sector when progressing towards the inclusive socio-economic development, as the present level and quality of energy supply are not adequate to support such high human development. Although there is tremendous technical resource potential, the level of commercial exploitation of RE for power generation in South Asia, particularly the new REs such as solar and wind, is not very significant yet. Heavy dependence on imported fossil fuels together with a single major source of supply have impacted energy security and economic stability of the countries. On the other hand, the lower level of energy consumption together with limited use of natural resources for economic output per capita suggest that there is a window of opportunity for establishing a policy framework to enable a paradigm shift in the energy sector through large-scale exploitation and commercialisation of REs to drive the nations towards much anticipated sustainable development. Accordingly, the central role of RE in the power sector has been recognised in the recent policy responses in all the countries, as signified in their NDCs.

Despite high resource potentials, drivers and multiple benefits, promotion of RE technologies and systems faces a host of challenges (including barriers and risks), ranging across several areas including policy and governance, technical, financial and market, and capacity and information, affecting the progress and lessening the potential benefits. Though there are some innovative policy responses and programmes initiated to address some of these barriers, more forward-looking policies and strategies are necessary to promote RE for electricity in South Asia, with emphasis on regional-level cooperation for knowledge-sharing and technology transfer.

End Notes

1. UN General Assembly, "Transforming Our World: The 2030 Agenda for Sustainable Development," resolution adopted by the UN General Assembly on September 25, 2015.
2. UN, "Sustainable Energy for All — A Framework for Action", The Secretary-General's High-level Group on Sustainable Energy for All, January, 2012,

accessed November 10, 2017, https://www.seforall.org/sites/default/files/l/2013/09/SE_for_All_-_Framework_for_Action_FINAL.pdf.

3.   The World Bank, "Sustainable Energy for All — Global Tracking Framework," Volume 3, Report Number 77889, http://documents.worldbank.org/curated/en/ 603241469672143906/pdf/778890GTF0full0report.pdf.

4.   IPCC, *Climate Change 2014: Mitigation of Climate Change, Working Group III Contribution to the Fifth Assessment Report of the Intergovernmental Panel on Climate Change* (New York: Cambridge University Press, 2014).

5.   UNFCCC, "Nationally Determined Contributions (NDCs),"accessed November 10, 2017, http://www4.unfccc.int/ndcregistry/Pages/All.aspx.

6.   Muhammad Iftikhar, Fatima Najeeb, Sardar Mohazzam and Shahida Khan, "Sustainable Energy for All in South Asia: Potential, Challenges, and Solutions,"Working Paper #151, Sustainable Development Policy Institute, June, 2015.

7.   ADB, "Energy Outlook for Asia and the Pacific," October, 2013, https://www.adb.org/sites/default/files/publication/ 30429/energy-outlook.pdf.

8.   The South Asia Regional Initiative for Energy Integration (SARI/EI), "Regional Energy Security for South Asia", Regional Report, South Asia Regional Initiative for Energy (SARI/Energy) Programme, 2006.

9.   The World Bank, "World Development Indicators Database," accessed February 20, 2018, https://data.worldbank.org/indicator.

10. UNDP, *Human Development Report 2016 — Human Development for Everyone* (New York: United Nations Development Programme, 2016).

11. The World Bank, "World Development Indicators Database."

12. UNDP, *Human Development Report 2016 — Human Development for Everyone*.

13. The World Bank, "World Development Indicators Database."

14. UNDP, *Human Development Report 2016 — Human Development for Everyone*.

15. V. K. Kharbanda, "Energy Integration in South Asia Region — Progress, Key Achievements and Way forward," in *HAPUA-UNESCAP Workshop*, April 17–19, 2017, Jakarta, Indonesia.

16. Centre for Science and Environment, "Global Renewable Energy Support Programme: Globally Funded Payment Guarantees/Feed-in Tariffs for Electricity Access through Renewable Sources," Discussion Paper (New Delhi: Centre for Science and Environment, 2015).

17. The World Bank, "World Development Indicators Database."

18. IEA, "Key World Energy Statistics," 2016.

19. UNDP, "Human Development Report 2015 — Work for Human Development," Statistical Annex, accessed February 20, 2018, http://hdr.undp.org/sites/default/files/hdr_2015_statistical _annex.pdf.

20. V. K. Kharbanda, "Energy Integration in South Asia Region — Progress, Key Achievements and Way forward."

21. Centre for Science and Environment, "Global Renewable Energy Support Programme: Globally Funded Payment Guarantees/Feed-in Tariffs for Electricity Access through Renewable Sources."

22. IPCC, *Climate Change 2013: The Physical Science Basis, Working Group I Contribution to the Fifth Assessment Report (AR5) of the Intergovernmental Panel on Climate Change* (UK, New York: Cambridge University Press, 2013).

23. WWF International, *Living Planet Report 2014: Species and Spaces, People and Places* (Gland, Switzerland: World Wide Fund International, 2014).

24. IPCC, *Climate Change 2013: The Physical Science Basis, Working Group I Contribution to the Fifth Assessment Report (AR5) of the Intergovernmental Panel on Climate Change.*

25. UNDP, *Human Development Report 2016 — Human Development for Everyone.*

26. WWF International, *Living Planet Report 2014: Species and Spaces, People and Places.*

27. *Ibid.*

28. The Ellen MacArthur Foundation, "Towards the Circular Economy — Economic and Business Rationale for an Accelerated Transition," Volume 1, 2013.

29. Muhammad Iftikhar, Fatima Najeeb, Sardar Mohazzam and Shahida Khan, "Sustainable Energy for All in South Asia: Potential, Challenges, and Solutions."

30. The South Asia Regional Initiative for Energy Integration (SARI/EI), "Energy Security for South Asia."

31. Akash Kumar Shukla, K. Sudhakar and Prashant Baredar, "Renewable Energy Resources in South Asian Countries: Challenges, Policy and Recommendations," *Resource-Efficient Technologies* 3(2017): 342–346.

32. Ram Manohar Shrestha, Mahfuz Ahmed, Suphachol Suphachalasai and Rodel Lasco, *Economics of Reducing Greenhouse Gas Emissions in South Asia: Options and Costs* (Manila: Asian Development Bank, 2012).

33. Shell Global, "Global Energy Resources Database," accessed February 25, 2018, https://www.shell.com/energy-and-innovation/the-energy-future/scenarios/shell-scenarios-energy-models/energy-resource-database.html.

34. *Ibid.*

35. *Ibid.*

36. V. K. Kharbanda, "Energy Integration in South Asia Region — Progress, Key Achievements and Way forward."

37. Ceylon Electricity Board, "Long-term Generation Expansion Plan 2018–2037," April, 2017.
38. V. K. Kharbanda, "Energy Integration in South Asia Region — Progress, Key Achievements and Way forward."
39. UNFCCC, "Nationally Determined Contributions (NDCs)."
40. *Ibid.*
41. Ram Manohar Shrestha, Mahfuz Ahmed, Suphachol Suphachalasai and Rodel Lasco, *Economics of Reducing Greenhouse Gas Emissions in South Asia: Options and Costs.*
42. Sultan Hafeez Rahman, Priyantha D. C. Wijayatunga, Herath Gunatilake and P. N. Fernando, *Energy Trade in South Asia — Opportunities and Challenges* (Manila: Asian Development Bank, 2011).
43. D. N. Raina, "SAARC Regional Energy Trade Study (SRETS)," Project No. 41125, Final Report, SAARC Secretariat, March, 2010.
44. Priyantha Wijayatunga and Tilak Siyambalapitiya, "Improving Energy Efficiency in South Asia," ADB South Asia Working Paper Series No. 47 (Manila: Asian Development Bank, 2016).
45. IndexMundi, "Electric Power Transmission and Distribution Losses (% of Output)," accessed February 25, 2018, https://www.indexmundi.com/facts/indicators/EG.ELC.LOSS.ZS/compare#country=af:bd:bt:in:np:pk:8s.
46. The Ellen MacArthur Foundation, "Towards the Circular Economy — Economic and Business Rationale for an Accelerated Transition."
47. W. D. A. G. K. Katugaha, K. A. C. Seneviratne, S. A. G. C. Subasinghe and A. G. T. Sugathapala, "Assessment of Renewable Energy Technologies using Multi-Criteria Decision-Analysis: Input to a RE Technology Road-Map," in *Vidulka National Energy Symposium 2014*, Sri Lanka Sustainable Energy Authority (SLSEA), November 19, 2014, BMICH, Colombo 07.
48. FS-UNEP Center, *Global Trends in Renewable Energy Investment 2017*, Frankfurt School — UNEP Collaborating Centre for Climate & Sustainable Energy Finance (FS-UNEP Center), (Frankfurt am Main: Frankfurt School of Finance & Management, 2017).
49. *Ibid.*
50. Akash Kumar Shukla, K. Sudhakar and Prashant Baredar, "Renewable Energy Resources in South Asian Countries: Challenges, Policy and Recommendations," 342–346.
51. Muhammad Iftikhar, Fatima Najeeb, Sardar Mohazzam and Shahida Khan, "Sustainable Energy for All in South Asia: Potential, Challenges, and Solutions."

Chapter 6

Transitioning Sustainability through Cross-border Energy Trade in South Asia

Riasat Noor

Introduction

Everything serving for the proving ground of energy cooperation can be found in South Asia[1]: growing energy demand with limited resources, steep economic boom and abundant clean energy. To meet its ever-increasing (4.6% per annum) energy demand, South Asia can achieve the required economic growth and further generate US$80 billion worth of intra-regional trade through energy connectivity and power trading. This can reduce increased dependence on import, and mass-scale emission of hydrocarbon derivatives. The trading atmosphere can enable cooperative engagement — offering robust regional stability, people-to-people contact and improved connectivity. The potential of energy trading can be exploited by building several technical infrastructures, such as: robust transmission network and regional power grid. At the institutional stage, cross-border energy trading needs adequate investment for its medium and long-term projects. At the same time, an inter-country coherent policy and regulatory framework can help remove institutional bottlenecks and reduce project lead time. If these required criteria are met and challenges are contained, South Asia can be a testament to how energy cooperation can maximise regional integration to unleash higher economic growth.

It is almost impossible to achieve low carbon energy transition, and ensure efficient and sustainable energy integration without appreciating the blessing of energy connectivity. It directly and indirectly designs our economic and regional development — starting with meeting the basic needs of decent lifestyle and goes beyond connecting the avant-garde human advancements that we can ever imagine. The emergence of low carbon energy transition is directly associated with energy efficient solutions, such as, smart and clean energy, availability of alternative fuels and energy trading options within the neighbouring countries. For the emerging countries, especially the South Asian economies, the necessity of energy trading platforms are much more important.

Energy Context: South Asia

Home to around 2 billion people, South Asia comprises of more than 23% of global population. However, this heavily populated region has an aggregated GDP of around US$2.9 trillion which is only 3.8% of the world GDP (US$75.642 trillion). This has resulted from weaker trade integration among the states. Although similar socio-economic background offers further scope of deeper regional integration and stronger trade and infrastructural network, this region has only 5.58% of intra-regional trade compared to 23.56% in Southeast Asia[2] and 62.92% in the EU.[3] Due to the lack of proper infrastructure and logistical service, intra-regional trade is more expensive than trading with external partners. For example, it is 20% cheaper for India to trade with Brazil than with its neighbour — Pakistan.[4] However, the region is having one of the fastest growing economic boom in the world at more than 7% GDP growth.

Looking into the power and energy context, we can see that South Asia is a solid ground of one of the most diversified and proven energy fields. In terms of sharable but unexploited and underexploited energy resources, South Asian geography offers a unique blend of hydrocarbon-based energy resources, e.g., natural gas, coal, oil; and clean energy sources, e.g., wind, solar and hydropower.

However, in terms of total energy consumption, there is a huge gap in demand and supply capacity of the region. For example, the region consumed 928.4 Million tonnes of oil equivalent (mtoe) in 2013, when the domestic production was only 641.7 mtoe. This leads to an increased dependence on import from foreign markets. In 2014, average electricity consumption in South Asia was 707 Kilowatt hour (kWh), as opposed to the world average of 3,128 kWh. It has the second lowest per capita electricity consumption in the world following Sub-Saharan Africa. Per capita CO_2 emission is considerably high and cities like Dhaka, and New Delhi are suffering from havoc wrecking smog — a result of increased industrialization and urbanization.[5] Sustenance of this phenomenal economic and industrial growth is met at the expense of environmental degradation, resulting in a 4.6% energy growth per annum — far exceeding the region's capacity to meet.[6]

At the Global Benchmarks[7]

South Asia has an average access to electricity of around 80%, whereas neighbouring regions, such as, East and Asia Pacific has 97%, and the Europe, Central Asia and North America has 100% access to electricity. South Asia has the second lowest per capita electricity consumption in the world. In both counts, only Sub-Saharan Africa has lower performance than South Asia. Electricity production from combustible renewable energy is negligible and average transmission and distribution loss is 18% in South Asia, whereas neighbouring Southeast Asia has 10% and EU has only 7.2% (Figure 1).[8]

General Benchmarking Criterion	South Asia	East and Asia Pacific	Sub-Saharan Africa	Europe & Central Asia	North America
Access to Electricity	80%	97%	37%	100%	100%
Per Capita Electricity Consumption (kWh)	707	3,680	483	6,592	13,243

Figure 1:   South Asia at global benchmarks.

Source: Author's analysis.

Table 1:   Energy trilemma performance in SA, SEA and EU (2017).

Region	Energy security	Energy equality	Environmental sustainability	Balance score
South Asia (SA)	84.5	99	71.75	98.25
Southeast Asia (SEA)	68.75	55	59.25	53
European Union (EU)	31.75	28.23	34.35	21.54

Note: Scores are indexed at reverse order: higher performance reflects top numbered categories, hence lower scores indicate higher performance.
Source: Author's analysis.

South Asian energy sector also falls behind the global performance when calculating economic growth and development, energy access and security and environmental sustainability. The index[9] shows that South Asia has an average of 0.54 (on a scale of 0 to 1), when Southeast Asia scored 0.59 and EU 0.70.[10]

There is increasing concern for energy security across South Asia due to rapidly growing energy demand and import dependence. Coupled with factors such as weather-related disruptions, this region continuously performs poor in the energy trilemma dimensions. The strong demand for energy also challenges environmental sustainability performance and increases energy supply risks. In order to solve the Energy Trilemma issue in South Asia, the region needs to ensure that the ever-increasing energy demand is met while improving energy access and resilience at the same time. Table 1[11] summarises energy trilemma performance in 2017[12]:

Need for Energy Cooperation in South Asia

South Asia faces energy crisis in most of its countries, with a unique need for energy cooperation — low electricity supply in Afghanistan, single fuel dominance in Bangladesh, limited electricity supply in Northern India, heavy import dependence in Maldives and Sri Lanka, seasonal blackouts in Nepal and underdeveloped renewable energy sector in Pakistan. As a whole, the region faces a burgeoning gap in energy supply and demand and inefficiency in the domestic markets.

Afghanistan is in dire need of electricity supply. Although, it has more than 70% electricity access, Afghanistan relies on 80% on imported power for almost 80% of its domestic need. Recently, the country has been connected to the CASA-1000 (Central Asia–South Asia power project) network to import hydroelectricity from Tajikistan and Kyrgyzstan in the winter seasons. However, the current import of 600 MW energy is not sufficient as Afghanistan will need around 3,000 MW to meet domestic demand by 2020. To meet the increasing domestic demand, Afghanistan imports additional energy from Uzbekistan, Turkmenistan and Iran.

Bangladesh will have to look for alternative energy sources by 2025 as it is primarily dependent on natural gas which is rapidly depleting. Its heavy dependence on imported fuel is attributing to unnecessary fiscal burden and environmental degradation. Although the country is developing a 2.4 GW nuclear power plant, it is expected to face similar power deficit for the next 10 years due to high system loss and erratic power supply.

Bhutan has abundant supply of seasonal hydropower generation — particularly in the months of May–September. India imports the surplus hydropower from Bhutan under the 2006 Inter-Governmental Treaty to support its energy-starved northern and northeastern parts and Bhutan imports electricity from India in the dry winters. However, this country has no oil and gas reserve.

India has several options for primary energy — coal (44%), biomass and waste (23%), petroleum products (23%) and natural gas (6%). To meet its diversified energy need, India has several bilateral and trilateral energy cooperation within the Bangladesh, Bhutan, India, Nepal (BBIN) network, i.e., Bangladesh (600 MW), Bhutan (1,450 MW) and Nepal (150 MW) to meet its rapidly booming economy. Still almost half of India's 1.3 billion people have no/limited access to electricity.

Maldives has no significant reserve for energy resources. For its domestic purpose, it is heavily dependent on imported oil and liquid fuel. For further sustenance, Maldives has plans to develop solar power system at large scale. The existing transmission networks are vulnerable to natural disasters as the country is frequently visited with torrential floods and wind storms from the Indian Ocean. Unfortunately, Maldives is not connected to the transmission lines with other South Asian countries.

In addition, due to the difficulty in acquiring long submarine cable links, it is not physically viable to establish power interconnections between Maldives and the rest of South Asia at the current stage.

Similar to Bhutan, Nepal has large hydropower resources but experiences severe power shortages and blackouts during the dry seasons. It is projected that the country will have exportable surplus hydropower during the monsoon seasons within the next 5 years. This will be exported to India and other BBIN states through the planned transmission lines of 1,000 MW (currently, 400 MW).

Although Pakistan has relatively underdeveloped renewable energy sector, it has access to large hydropower resources. However, the country has severe power shortage and supply shortfall. Similar to Afghanistan, Pakistan has been connected to the CASA-1000 network to import surplus hydroelectric power from Central Asian countries.

Sri Lanka is heavily dependent on imported liquid fuels and has plans to develop large coal power plants. However, domestic cost of power is extremely high due to high import. To meet rising energy crisis, Sri Lankan government is initiating solar-based power options, which can meet around 32% of its annual domestic demand of 10,500 GW. Only 0.01% of this potential is operational and the government is aiming to feed 220 MW solar power to the national transmission grid by 2020. Alike Maldives, Sri Lanka is detached from possible power trade with other South Asian economies due to the absence of transmission network.[13]

South Asia, in general is crippled with archaic power sharing apparatus with an ever-increasing energy demand. This breeds the need for public and private investment to help:

- Properly optimise existing resources and transact power through transmission lines.
- Manage daily demand variations and peak requirements through Day-Ahead Transactions.
- Move from single fuel dominant region to highly responsive and diversified market.
- Produce standardised contracts and competitive prices module. This will eliminate the need for negotiations.

Existing Energy Trade in South Asia

South Asian countries are trading power bilaterally and regionally since the 1970s with the formulation of the bilateral river treaty in 1972 and subsequently, long-term Power Purchase Agreement (PPA) between Bangladesh and India. As the post millennia energy crisis is brewing, the region's daily and seasonal load diversity can be a good case for deeper energy integration. The region has potential for energy sharing that can be exercised both within and outside of the neighbouring regions. Currently, limited bilateral electricity trade takes place within the BBIN network (Bangladesh, Bhutan, India and Nepal) with little/no energy trade in energy resources, i.e., coal, gas and oil.

Bhutan

Government-to-government power trading with the Indian PTC consists of three long-term projects at Chukka, Kurichhu and Tala.

- Connectivity via multiple A/C links with India:
  - ○ Chukha HEP (4×84 MW) through Chukha–Birpara 220 kV line;
  - ○ Radial loads at Indian border through Bongaigaon–Geylegphug 132 kV line;
  - ○ Kurichu HEP (4×15 MW) through Geylegphug–Salakati 132 kV line;
- Export of 1,020 MW (by six 170-MW generators) power through Tala Hydroelectric Project to India (Bhutan aims to export 10,000 MW by 2020).

Bangladesh

- 400 kV Double Circuit (D/C) Line at Baharampur–Bheramara transmission line, 400 kV switching station at Baharampur which is complemented by another 500 MW High-Voltage, Direct Current (HVDC) line at the Bheramara sub-station (400/230 kV);
- 100 MW from Tripura (India) to Comilla (Bangladesh);
- Agreement between Power Grid (India) and BPDB (Bangladesh);
- Agreement between Powerlinks (India) and Power Grid (Bangladesh).

Nepal

- Connectivity via 3×132 kV lines and 8×33 kV lines;
- Development of two Joint Ventures (JV): 400 kV Muzaffarpur (India) and Dhalkebar (Nepal);
- Agreement with India to construct a 40-km pipeline to transport petroleum products from India to Nepal.

Power Trading with India

India exports grid connected electricity to Bangladesh. Although the current trading is limited to 600 MW of electricity, these neighbours are

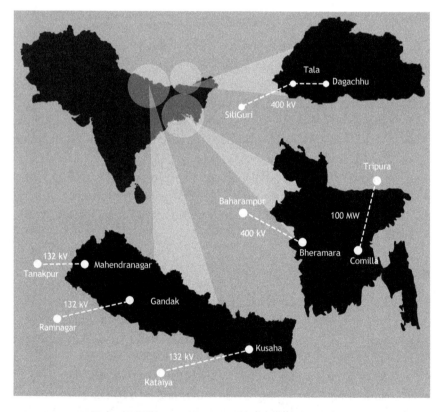

Figure 2:   Energy connectivity (partial) in South Asia.
Source: Author's compilation.

looking for diversifying energy-trading baskets at different capacities. Bangladeshi state-owned BPDB is importing 250 MW of electricity from India through NTPC and another privatised 250 MW through PTC. Another G2G powered 100 MW connectivity has also been established between Tripura and Comilla.

Figure 2 shows the energy cooperation routes between India and other countries. India exports 350 MW of hydro to Nepal through cross-country lines. Among this, 25 MW is carried through Ramnagar–Gandak lines, 30 MW through Tanakpur–Mahendranagar and the remaining 120 MW through Dhalkebar–Muzaffarpur transmission line. This route is under development to house a total of 280 MW handling capacity. Recently, another 20–30 MW of electricity was extracted from the Tanakpur–Mahendranagar line to reduce constant power outage.[14]

In addition to electricity trading, there are limited exports of diesel from India to Bangladesh and trade of petroleum products at piecemeal stages between India and Bangladesh, Bhutan to Sri Lanka, and Nepal to Sri Lanka (via the northeastern regions of India).

Current and Envisaged Inter-Regional Energy Trade

Although South Asia has several trans-regional power-trading platforms with resource-rich Central Asia, most of these initiatives are not fully operational. Turkmenistan–Afghanistan–Pakistan–India (TAPI) gas pipeline is being developed for many years now, Iran-Pakistan-India (IPI) Gas Pipeline is struggling with geopolitical dilemma, while Myanmar–Bangladesh–India gas pipeline stalls at the planning stage. The current inter-regional electricity trade is limited to Afghanistan importing power from Central Asian Republic (CARs) and Pakistan from Iran.

TAPI gas pipeline

The 1,814-km Turkmenistan–Afghanistan–Pakistan–India Pipeline (TAPI) Pipeline is known as the Trans-Afghanistan Pipeline and expected to be commercialised by 2019. Once commissioned, this gas pipeline will be able to syphon natural gas from the Caspian Sea and transfer from Turkmenistan to Pakistan and India via Afghanistan and then to India.

Dubbed as the modern continuation of the Silk Road, TAPI gas pipeline will be able to counterbalance Russian dominance in the region and export energy to the South Asian countries.

Russia–China–India pipeline

The Russia–China–India (RCI) Pipeline was introduced in 2003 for the Eurasian energy market that links Afghanistan, Ladakh (India), and Pakistan with Kazakhstan, Russia, Turkmenistan, Uzbekistan, and Xinjiang (China). In 2016, India and Russia discussed to extend the pipeline by pouring a fresh US$25 billion investment.[15]

CASA-1000

CASA-1000 is another success story that connects the Central Asian energy market with the South Asian energy deficit states. As Pakistan and Afghanistan's domestic power outage and shortage are still unmanageable, power sharing within the CASA-1000 network is the best viable route to tap in necessary energy resources and tackle load-shedding. This transmission line will be trading hydropower electricity through high voltage transmission infrastructure between Kyrgyzstan and Tajikistan (477 km) and from Tajikistan to Afghanistan and Pakistan (750 km). Opening in 2016, this project is planned to be fully operationalised after June 2020. This network is now currently focusing on providing 1,300 MW electricity in Pakistan, as Afghanistan's demand for electricity has recently plummeted.

Iran–Pakistan (IP) gas pipeline

This proposed 2,775-km "Peace pipeline" will transfer natural gas from South Pars gas field (Iran) to Multan (Pakistan). Initially the project included India which would be a beneficiary from Iranian gas, but completion of the long-stalled project is now uncertain due to geopolitical complexity. India has backed off from the project due to over pricing and security issues, Saudi Arabia is pressurizing Pakistan to not ramp up further ties with Iran, Iran is pushing Pakistan to put in a fresh bid, Russia is pouring infrastructure investment and US is imposing unilateral sanctions for the IP gas pipeline.[16]

Key Developments in Cross-Border Trading

Development of the BBIN network and signing of South Asian Association for Regional Cooperation (SAARC) framework agreement on energy cooperation were two major milestones for energy trading that welcomed several energy sharing agreements and platforms in South Asia — the following are a few till date[17]:

- **SAARC Framework Agreement on Energy (Electricity) Cooperation:** With a vision to provide non-discriminatory access to the SAARC countries, SAARC Framework Agreement for Energy cooperation (electricity) was signed in 2014. The agreement provided guidelines for institutional and regulatory mechanism for promoting cross-border energy/electricity trading (CBET) in the region. This framework enabled exemption of export–import and custom duties for cross-border energy trading and provision of electricity exchange between buying and selling entities.[18]
- **SARPEX Mock Exercise:** SARPEX is a concept of a power exchange platform for power trade between the South Asian Nations which is currently applicable to Bangladesh, Bhutan, India and Nepal due to existing grid connectivity among these countries. The concept was exercised at a stakeholder consultation workshop in June 2017 to substantiate the feasibility of regional power grid.[19]
- **Inter-Governmental Agreement Bhutan and India:** The inter-governmental agreement between Bhutan and India was marked in April 2014. This agreement concentrated on the development of hydropower plants for mutual benefits with support from public and private organizations. This framework also provided guidelines for developing four major hydropower projects in Bhutan at Bunakha, Chamkharchu, Kholongchhu and Wangchu totalling 2,120 MW.[20]
- **Power Trade Agreement (India and Nepal):** India and Nepal inked the Power Trade Agreement (PTA) in September 2014. This agreement targeted at exploring and identifying existing and new areas of

cooperation in the power sector with a focus in hydropower. Under this agreement, Nepal will focus on exporting excess power in the wet season and importing during the dry season to India, as it has the capacity of seasonal electricity generation.

Potential of Energy Cooperation

Looking at some of the key facts, South Asia has massive unutilised energy potential (Figure 3, Author's analysis from different sources):

Further breakdown of the energy potential shows estimated energy resource endowment for the designated countries[21,22] (Table 2):

The hilly area extending 2-km at the Indian Meghalaya state borders with northeastern Bangladesh. Aside from having huge hydro reserve, these neighbouring countries can trade the derivatives of natural gas. Recently, Indian ONGC has discovered a huge gas deposit in Tripura state,

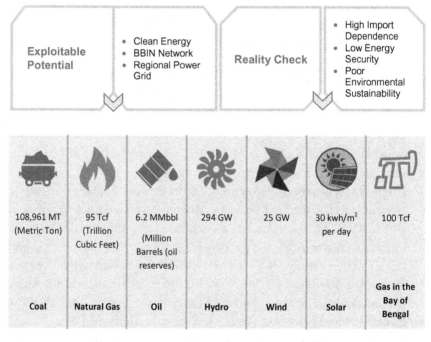

Figure 3: Unexplored energy potential in South Asia.
Source: Author's compilation from various sources.

Table 2: Energy resource endowment in South Asia.

Country	Coal (MT)	Natural gas (TCF)	Oil (MB)	Hydropower[23] (GW)	Biomass (GW)
Afghanistan	440	15	Not Available	25	18–27
Bhutan	2	0	0	30	26.6
Bangladesh	884	8	12	0.33	0.08
India	90,085	39	5,700	150	139
Maldives	0	0	0	0	0.06
Nepal	Not Available	0	0	83	27.04
Pakistan	17,550	33	324	59	Not Available
Sri Lanka	Not Available	0	150	2	12
Total	**108,961**	**95**	**6,186**	**349.33**	**223**

Source: Author's projection.

adjacent to the eastern borders of Bangladesh. Currently, the company has targeted to unearth 5 Million Metric Standard Cubic meter per day (MMSCMD) gas by mid-2018. This region houses the Palatana Combined Cycle Gas Turbine (CCGT) with a capacity of 726.6 MW. This gas-based power plant is adjacent to the gas fields in Tripura and complementing electricity supply to the energy-deficit seven sisters of the North Eastern India and 100 MW to Bangladesh. The current expansion plan of ONGC includes more gas mining from the Tripura reserve that can be transferred to Bangladesh. This follows the possibility of another 500–1,000 MW power exchange from 2020.[24,25] Already, the two governments are in talks to finalise the 765 kV transmission capacity mounting from Assam to the northeastern part of India, crossing Bangladesh (Bornagar–Parbatipur–Katihar), which will be a beneficiary in the process. This transmission line will be far more important than electricity transmission, as it will be able to direct Bhutan's excess hydroelectricity to India and Bangladesh.[26]

Opportunities in hydropower

South Asia has several excellent options of renewable and clean energy that can be tapped or replicated into other states, especially within the BBIN network. For example, both Bhutan and Nepal can trade hydroelectricity with India and Bangladesh. As these upstream countries have surplus electricity generation in the months of May to September, downstream countries with significant energy deficit, such as, India and Bangladesh can tap into the opportunity. Similarly, India can be the hub of energy cooperation and Bhutan can export hydropower to Bangladesh via India. Installing only 1.6 GW of hydro, Bhutan has developed only 5% of its total hydropower potential of 30 GW, with 23.8 GW techno-economically exploitable.[27] With the support of India's technical and financial assistance programs, Bhutan has implemented several hydropower projects like Chukha (336 MW), Krichu (60 MW) and Tala (1,020 MW). Alike Bhutan, Nepal has exploitable hydropower potential of 44 GW. This surplus hydroelectricity of Bhutan and Nepal is exportable to Bangladesh, India and Pakistan during the monsoon seasons of May–September.

India has huge potential to capitalise on its hydro potential. In fact, it has over 90 GW of pumped storage potential, with only 49 GW of installed capacity. In addition, Assam has the huge coal and hydro reserve in northeastern India.[28,29]

Bangladesh can utilise the thermal and hydro potential from Bhutan, India and Nepal to meet its growing electricity demand. Considering the potential interconnection with its neighbouring countries, Bangladesh has incorporated a long-term transmission plan in its Power System Master Plan (PSMP).

Replicable opportunities in small scale wind energy

For solar power option, South Asian economies can look into Solar Home System (SHS)-based applications. As the tropic of cancer directly crosses over the region, it has the potential of generating and capturing massive daylight that can be converted into solar power. In this case, SHS can be successfully replicated into other South Asian countries. Bangladesh has produced some of the best works in this case. The fastest growing solar-based installation in the world is suitable for off grid and inaccessible areas of the South Asian countries. This method can be used for clean cooking and solar-based irrigation in rural areas, where proper electrification is not possible.

Installation of wind turbines, usually operated in remote areas covers complex terrains such as urban and suburban areas. Small scale wind towers and turbines are ideal for disintegrated islands and unreachable hill tracts with no access to electric grid.

The island countries, i.e., Maldives and Sri Lanka are ideal for replicating the application of small scale wind turbines in South Asia. Depending on imported liquid fuels, Sri Lanka has no power trade with any of the South Asian countries, and the government is trying to replicate a wind-based energy model. Similarly, most of the islands in Maldives have energy demand under 500 kW — this is particularly practical to develop smaller wind turbines and hybrid plants. This is perfect for hybrid wind-diesel and wind-solar systems in the country.

The low tariff hybrid modules from Croatia and Germany can be successfully replicated in Maldives and Sri Lanka. Moreover, the coastal areas of Indian Ocean, i.e., India, Maldives and Sri Lanka already have 25 GW of wind potential. The fallow lands of the coastal areas can generate 30 Kwh/m² of solar power per day.

The cost effective models of the small scale wind turbines (1–100 kW) can range from US$2,100 to 3,500.

Opportunities in regional power grid

South Asian countries have dynamic seasonal and daily load curves. This scenario requires optimizable energy sources which can be exploited by tapping into the potential for cross border power exchanges. To minimise import dependence and optimise existing regional resources, few exploitable options for regional power grid are mentioned as follows:

- Due to their high domestic demand, Bangladesh and India can import power from Bhutan and Nepal as they have surplus generation in the summer.
- Due to its geographically convenient location, India can utilise its transmission system towards proper power wheeling between BBIN countries and impose wheeling charges.
- For the same reason, India can allow transit rights for constructing a designated power-trading transmission system in the region.
- Power exchange between India and Pakistan can meet electricity demand of the energy-starved states at borders. Such arrangements

will reduce further investment requirements, improve reserve margin, lower transmission losses and enhance supply reliability.

- A central regional gas grid will help the SA countries obtain gas from Central Asia, Myanmar and West Asia. Although in limited application, several bilateral and multilateral gas pipelines are already in application stage. Conceived proposals such as, Iran–Pakistan–India (IPI) pipeline will be able to transport 2.8 billion cubic feet/day (bcf/day) of gas from Iran's South Pars natural gas fields to India across Pakistan. Similarly, Turkmenistan–Afghanistan–Pakistan–India (TAPI) will be capable of transporting natural gas from Central Asian countries to South Asia.

Roadblocks of Energy Trading in South Asia

Although South Asia has vast unexploited potential in energy, some roadblocks have been deterring the journey of energy sharing.

Lack of centralised power market, synchronised and robust interconnection facilities, and proper transmission network results in poor energy transaction among the states in South Asia. For example, the required high-voltage direct current (HVDC) interconnection cost of every 500 MW bloc is around US$239 million within India, Bangladesh, Nepal and Bhutan. Other than technical challenges, the region has some unresolved policy and institutional issues. Lack of trust and cooperation generated from political and historical tussles have failed the region to offer any uniform platform that can offer adequate capacity building programs. Even the institutional bottlenecks and inter-departmental conflicts within the countries have discouraged the foreign investors to provide fund for the long-term projects. Lack of intra-country coherent policy framework is another factor deterring the intra-regional energy trade.

Some of the long-standing challenges for South Asian energy cooperation are as follows:

- Absence of proper infrastructure and adaptive power market;
- Technical barriers, i.e., synchronization of grid system and grid codes to electric power and natural gas pipeline technology;
- Lack of funding mechanism and investment priorities;
- Lack of requisite energy infrastructure for developing hydro projects;

- Environmental issues involving construction of multipurpose projects;
- Lack of harmonious energy policy and related framework,
- Institutional bottlenecks and lack of inter-departmental cohesion;
- Divergent political mindset to energy trade;
- History of mistrust and non-cooperation; and
- Expensive Operations & Maintenance (O&M) utilities.

These factors eventually impact overall regional synergy and indicators related to energy performance:

- Single fuel dominant economy;
- Rising import dependency;
- Unrealised energy potential;
- Unutilised cross-border energy trading; and
- Poor regional synergy and growth.

Forming Deeper Regional Integration through Energy Cooperation

South Asia can guarantee greater regional integration if it exploits the options of cross-border energy trading. Some of the presumed benefit of the energy cooperation are as follows:

- **Improved Connectivity:** It may open doors for connectivity in areas like transport, cyber space and people-to-people connectivity resulting in increased bilateral and multilateral trade. Although BBIN was institutionalised in 2015, it has failed to grab full potential of connectivity. As shown before, South Asia has the potential of augmented energy trading within the BBIN network. If properly implemented, this platform can bridge the gap in infrastructure cooperation, transport connectivity and trans-shipment of goods.
- **Reduced Carbon Emission:** Hydropower sharing can be a suitable option to achieving carbon free and pollution free environment in South Asia. If Bangladesh and India can tap into the hydropower option of Bhutan and Nepal, they can drastically reduce CO_2 emission and reduce dependence on rapidly depleting hydrocarbon resources, such as, gas and coal.

- **Energy Exchange and Sharing Platform:** Energy exchange and sharing platforms will reduce increased dependency on import. This liberalised power trading market will introduce synchronised power and grid connectivity — offering diversified power options and exchange platforms.
- **Regional Stability:** Most importantly, energy cooperation will offer harmonised and cohesive intra-regional integration through hallmark platforms, such as, SAARC, South Asian Free Trade Area (SAFTA) and Bay of Bengal Initiative for Multi-Sectoral Technical and Economic Cooperation (BIMSTEC). This will promote greater stability and peaceful cooperation within the region.
- **"Rely on Each Other":** With enough power options, the South Asian countries will be able to access cheaper energy sources. Tapping into the surplus generation from the neighbouring countries will enable diversification of energy sources and less dependence on primary energy source.

Cost–Benefit Value of Interconnection

If we look into the math, potential interconnectivity in the region proves much promising in every aspect. Figure 4 is a Cost–Benefit Analysis (CBA) of power and energy interconnectivity in the region. The simulation was prepared by ADB that shows that if the South Asian Countries can exploit the options of bilateral trading with its neighbouring countries, the annualised benefit can far exceed the investment cost of the interconnections. This can be exercised onto the near-term cross-border interconnections of most of the South Asian countries. This simulation has considered the utilisable interconnections that are already operational, yet to be commissioned, or even waiting at planning stage. The cost–benefit analysis shows that benefit-to-cost ratios are promisingly high, with a yield ranging from 3.7 to 102.

The considered interconnections are as follows:

- Additional grid reinforcement for hydropower evacuation from Bhutan to India;
- India–Nepal 400 kV transmission sub-stations at Dhalkebar, Butwal and Hetauda (Nepal) are operational;
- Proposed sub-sea transmission network at India-Sri Lanka HVDC connectivity that includes a 50-km submarine cable component;

Case	Capacity Particular	Interconnection cost (US\$, mn)	Benefit in 2016-17 (US\$, mn)	Benefit-to-Cost Ratio
India-Bhutan Grid Reinforcement	• 3,066 MW (3*1022 MW Hydro Projects)	• 140-160 (Total) • 18-20 (Annualised)	1,840	92-102
Nepal-India 400 kV Link	• 2,000 MW (Surplus State) • 650 MW (Deficit State)	• 186 (Total) • 20 (Annualised)	105	5.2 (Surplus) 10.7 (Deficit)
India-Sri Lanka HVDC Interconnection	• 630 MW (Coal) • 400 MW (Hydro)	• 339 (Total) • 50 (Annualised)	186	3.7
India-Bangladesh HVDC Link	-	• 192-250 (Total) • 25 (Annualised)	145-389	5.8-15.6

India-Pakistan 220 and 400 kV Link	• Short term
	  ○ 250 MW transfer (220 kV)
	• Medium and long term
	  ○ 500 MW transfer (400 kV)
		• Short term
		  ○ 50 (Total)
		  ○ 6 (Annualised)
		• Medium and long term
		  ○ 150 (Total)
		  ○ 18 (Annualised)
			451	55.8 (Short term)
				27.2 (Medium and long term)

Figure 4:   Cost–benefit values of interconnection.

Source: Author's customised analysis from ADB simulation.

- Bangladesh–India (Baharampur–Bheramara) HVDC transmission link; and
- India–Pakistan 220 and 400 kV transmission link.

   Capacity of each of these transmission interconnections varies from 250 to 2,100 MW and construction cost ranges from US$140 to 1,000 million.[30] If formulised, these interconnections will allow the candidates to optimally utilise existing utilities and resources to satisfy energy demand across the region. This is a unique illustration that shows that the South Asian landlocked countries can achieve maximum benefit through minimum interventions in energy cooperation.

Trailblazers of Energy Cooperation

South Asia has room for improvement against its minimal energy cooperation. It can take lessons from the success stories from different regions. Although South Asia is in dire need of energy for its economic growth, the region is still immature to embrace the full potential of energy cooperation. Although different regions have unique energy needs, the common practices of energy cooperation from outer regions can be customised to the South Asian context and replicated to its individual need. Three such cases are as follows:

Exhibit A: Nord Pool Spot

This European energy exchange market is the largest electricity trading platform in the world. Nord Pool Spot started as a joint Power Exchange (PX) platform headed by Sweden and Norway in 1996. More than 80% of total electrical energy consumption in the Nordic market is traded through Nord Pool. Established in 1991, this is the world's first multinational exchange platform for trading electric power that provides reliable power price to the customers. It has a total of 380 active members trading from 20 countries and operates Day-Ahead Markets (DAM) and Intra-Day Markets (IDM) in UK and the Nordic/Baltic countries. This platform can provide timely and accurate information to its daily liquid electricity exchange of around 1 TWh to the market. At the same time, Nord Pool brings together the energy companies and producers, brokers, TSO's and consumers in the energy market.

Exhibit B: South African Power Pool (SAPP)

South African Power Pool (SAPP) is a power and utility trading market that provides a uniform forum for regional solutions to electric and energy problems in the rural areas of the 12 Southern African countries. Most recently, the power pool is attracting foreign investments due to its resilient growth, and sound economic, environmental and social practices. With the objective of increasing power accessibility in the rural communities, this trading mechanism has recently achieved significant growth and successfully meeting most of the yearly energy consumption of 400 TWh. Recently, the market has recorded an increased trade volume in October compared to September in 2017. This has experienced a sharp 15.4% increase in the Day Ahead Markets (DAM), and 47.7% increase in the IDM transaction.

Exhibit C: European Power Exchange (EPEX Spot)

Dubbed as the heart of power trading in Europe, EPEX Spot covers short-term electricity trading in Austria, Belgium, France, Germany, United Kingdom, Luxembourg, Switzerland and the Netherlands. It enables electricity producers, trading organizations and consumers to exchange power and balance their demand and supply of energy. The EPEX platform provides both day-ahead and intra-day market along with other derivatives and follows market-based integration that facilitates excellent customer service. The Paris-based PX platform is now rendering modules for augmented customer support and exploring opportunities to expand beyond Europe. In 2016, the EPEX market amounted 529 TWh of electricity trading with 1,200 TWh of yearly power consumption, representing 50% of the European Union's integrated electricity market.[31]

The CBET Roadmap

South Asia can achieve elevated regional integration and further cooperation in trade, infrastructure, and connectivity through cooperation in power and energy. The once mass-traded avenues, such as, the Silk

Routes and modern connectivity platforms, such as, BBIN and BIMSTEC networks can utilise the existing resource pool through a well-planned energy roadmap. This roadmap (Figure 5) incorporates past areas of concentration, current scenario and proposed areas of cooperation. These can encompass a 360 degree of considerations ranging from policy perspective to technical parameters, soft issues such as tying the political memoranda to hard infrastructure such as focusing on grid synchronization and so on. Some of the non-exhaustive recommendations are as follows:

Capacity building and engagement

A platform for knowledge sharing, technical and instrumental training is essential in disseminating regional best practices and applications of energy trading. This platform can be the hub of interaction for local counterparts, academic, policy makers and technical institutes. Several capacity building training modules have been adopted at institutional level in this regard. The SARPEX Mock Exercise conceived by the USAID and SARI/EI has laid ground for power exchange platform in the region. Another similar program — SAARC Regional Energy Trade Study (SRETS) was conducted by ADB in 2010 that focused on energy trading potential in the region. The study also emphasised on conducting feasibility studies of developing transnational projects on electricity, coal and natural gas. Although conducted at piecemeal stages, these projects lack the initiative of undertaking technology-wise study, such as lignite use and equipment manufacture for coal-based power generation plants as well as renewable energy technology.

Creation of SA regional electricity market

It is highly recommended to establish a network for stable and reliable energy connectivity. The regional electricity market will have to be designed prudently, to ensure a level playing field for all nations and addressing concerns of all the participating nations including apprehension regarding the impact on the domestic market. This will provide uninterrupted power supply to the grid, prevent seasonal blackouts and provide a synchronised connectivity platform for effective electricity trading. In addition, a well-coordinated cross-border energy trading and sharing platform can help develop strategy frameworks that will be able to model scenarios and project, emulate and simulate cases for country-wise and region-wise cases. The energy exchange market can include both day-ahead and intra-day markets, which are ideal for short-term and long-term electricity trading in the region.

Coherent policy framework

South Asian countries are blessed with similar policy mechanisms. Especially for the trade and infrastructure frameworks, there are several institutional frameworks and policy instruments, such as, BIMSTEC, SAFTA and SAPTA. For power and energy connectivity, however, South Asia needs an intra-governmental policy framework conducive to easier energy trade and industry-friendly energy sharing environment. In this regard, a centralised regulatory authority should be adopted as early as possible.

The following regulatory issues should be covered in the policy framework:

- A single coordinated window amongst various ministries and departments;
- Synchronised grid code and operations and maintenance (O&M) procedure to operate on real-time parameters for multiple countries;
- Synchronised grids interconnection, in terms of — voltage, frequency, stability and reliability;
- Adoption of synchronised tariff mechanism.

Rebuilt regional dynamics

Sometimes promising not to engage further territorial conflict can be as important as avoiding one to understand mutual benefit. As much as we talk about the power trading, it is not possible to share energy without sharing the common regional interests. The long-standing history of political turmoil, ethnic and religious clashes, inefficient and inadequate conjoint initiatives among the member countries kept the potential of

Roadmap Priorities	Past Areas of Focus	Current Scenario	Proposed Areas of Focus
01 Regulatory Framework	–	• Framework for bilateral energy cooperation: e.g., SAARC framework agreement on energy (electricity). • Regulatory framework for PPAs: e.g., SAARC Council of Experts of Energy Regulators.	• SA Electricity Treaty; • Coordinated CBET Framework. • Trilateral CBET Policy Governing Frameworks.

02
 	
Soft and Hard Infrastructure
	• Hardware issues: technical and operational;
	• Software issues: e.g., transmission pricing;
		• Transmission interconnection: bilateral and multilateral.	• Grid Code sync;
			• Non-discriminatory open access in transmission;
			• Econometric Modelling;
			• Scheduling and load dispatching in real time;
			• Network power system analysis for
			  • BBIN
			  • India-Sri Lanka
			  • West Grid (Pak–Afg).

03 Business and Institutional	• Commercial trading arrangements. • Business case for cross-border energy trade: enabling policies, scenario modelling; • Analysis, institutional platform, investment mobilization.	• Framework for risk mitigation strategies (SAARC Framework Agreement for Energy Cooperation)	• Political consensus; • Investor forum for exploring CBET opportunity; • Regional settlement mechanism; • Tailored risk guarantees; • Usability of trading license, congestion management, grant of connectivity etc.
04 Capacity Building	• Knowledge sharing and allocation of availability resources; • Determination of available capacity; • SAARC Regional Energy Trade Study (SRETS).	• Conferences, Workshops, Webinar, and Technical Sessions; • Mock Exercise (SARPEX).	• Soft training relating to operational hurdles and conflict management; • Monitoring and compliance mechanism.

Figure 5:   The CBET roadmap.

Source: Author's compilation.

energy sharing mostly untapped. In this regard, a better understanding of peacebuilding, respect and mutual tolerance towards diversified regional cultural, political and ethno-sectorial background is important to promote opportunities for mutual benefits such as: energy sharing, cross border electricity trading, grid sharing and so on.

Investment and trade license regimes

It is equally important to focus on real time utilization of existing assets, transmission and generation and consumption framework. Each country of the region has different investment needs and priorities. However, for a synchronised cross-border energy trading, a region-centric investment prioritization is needed that can provide local incentives such as financial and technical assistance, grants and loans, i.e., for hydropower potential in Nepal and Bhutan electricity. For example, it will cost US$10–12 billion over 10–11 years to develop additional 10 GW of hydro capacity by 2020.[32] This will encourage the local counterparts and investors to reinvest in newer projects. This can be bolstered by institutionalizing trading licenses and developing investor-friendly environment in South Asia. India has well-functioning trading license regimes, while Bhutan's legal framework is developing its trading regime as a licensed activity. Other than Bhutan and India, no South Asian country has well-developed electricity-trading regime.[33]

Looking Forward

South Asia cannot have tailor-made solutions for each of its states to minimise the energy crisis. This becomes even truer with its promising economic growth. To unload the huge burden on energy import and to move towards a diversified portfolio of energy options, the best approach is to share the unutilised energy resources with the neighbours. This region has limitless possibility of enjoying the development dynamics through utilizing the interconnected energy market and capitalizing on geographic proximity and shared historical ties that can be translated into inclusive development and a deeper flow of engagement and integration among the states.

Power trading and energy cooperation can be the first step of ensuring this regional integration.

End Notes

1. South Asia comprises Afghanistan, Bangladesh, Bhutan, India, Maldives, Nepal, Pakistan and Sri Lanka.

2. Southeast Asia here comprises Brunei Darussalam, Cambodia, Indonesia, Lao, Malaysia, Myanmar, Philippines, Singapore, Thailand and Vietnam.
3. Asian Development Bank. *Asia Regional Integration Center* (2017). Retrieved from https://aric.adb.org/integrationindicators#.
4. World Bank. (2016, May 24). *The Potential of Intra-regional Trade for South Asia.* Retrieved from http://www.worldbank.org/en/news/infographic/2016/05/24/the-potential-of-intra-regional-trade-for-south-asia.
5. US Air Quality Index (AQI). (2018, January 31). *Air Pollution in World: Real-time Air Quality Index Visual Map.* Retrieved from Air Quality Index: http://aqicn.org/map/world/#@g/15.8719/94.5923/5z.
6. Noor, R. *Deep-Water Hydrocarbon in South Asia: Hunting at The Bay.* Retrieved from Energy & Power (2018). http://ep-bd.com/view/details/article/MTc0NQ%3D%3D/title?q=deep-water+hydrocarbon+in+south+asia%3A+hunting+at+t.
7. Footnote 3.
8. World Bank. *Electric power consumption (kWh per capita).* Retrieved from World Bank Data (2014). https://data.worldbank.org/indicator/EG.USE.ELEC.KH.PC.
9. Author's analysis from Global Energy Architecture Performance Index (EAPI) 2017.
10. World Economic Forum. *Global Energy Architecture Performance Index 2017* (Geneva: WEF, 2017).
11. Author's analysis from World Energy Trilemma Index 2017.
12. World Energy Council. (2017). *World Energy Trilemma Index 2017.* London: World Energy Council.
13. Perera, A. *High Costs Slowing Sri Lanka Push Toward Solar Energy.* Retrieved from Reuters (2016). https://www.reuters.com/article/us-srilanka-solar-energy/high-costs-slowing-sri-lanka-push-toward-solar-energy-idUSKCN11S0BE.
14. Gulati, M. *Powering India — Nepal Ties.* Retrieved from Centre for Land Warfare Studies (2017). http://www.claws.in/1743/powering-india-nepal-ties-monish-gulati.html.
15. "India, Russia to Study Construction of Gas Pipeline Costing $25 Billion". Retrieved from *Hindustan Times* (2016). https://www.hindustantimes.com/india-news/india-russia-to-study-construction-of-gas-pipeline-costing-25-billion/story-3vW5HFqAHTpMuCm8V9BcXM.html.
16. Bhutta, Z. "Iran Wants Pakistan to Revive Gas Pipeline Project". Retrieved from *The Express Tribune* (2017a). https://tribune.com.pk/story/1540538/

2-amid-saudi-arabia-us-pressure-iran-wants-pakistan-revive-gas-pipeline-project/ and Bhutta, Z. "US Backs Russian Investment in Iran–Pakistan Gas Pipeline". Retrieved from *The Express Tribune* (2017b) https://tribune.com.pk/story/1583457/2-us-backs-russian-investment-iran-pakistan-gas-pipeline/.

17. S.K. Ray and G. Jain. *Review & Key activities of South Asian Regional Power Exchange (SARPEX)* (USAID, 2016).

18. SASEC Asia. *SAARC Framework Agreement for Energy Cooperation Endorsed by Nepal Parliament*. Retrieved from SASEC (2016). https://www.sasec.asia/index.php?page=news&nid=516&url=saarc-framework-agreement-for-energy-cooperation.

19. SARI/EI. (2017a). Key Findings of the SARI/EI Study. *Stakeholder Consultation Meeting*. scheduling: SARI/EI.

20. *Bhutan-India Hydropower Relations*. Retrieved from MFA.GOV.BT (2017). http://www.mfa.gov.bt/rbedelhi/?page_id=28.

21. *Energy Trade in South Asia: Opportunities and Challenges* (Manila: ADB, 2012).

22. SARI/EI. (2014). *Cross-Border Electricity Trade in South Asia: Challenges and Investment Opportunities*. New Delhi: SARI/EI.

23. Estimated hydro-electric potential of South Asia is only 294.33 GW due to lower estimates for Pakistan, and Nepal (*Energy Trade in South Asia: Opportunities and Challenges* (Manila: ADB, 2012)).

24. Technology, P. (n.d.). *ONGC Tripura Power Plant*. Retrieved from Power Technology: https://www.power-technology.com/projects/ongc-tripura-power-plant/.

25. The Indian Express. (2017). *ONGC intensifies exploration of gas in Tripura*. Retrieved from The Indian Express: http://indianexpress.com/article/india/ongc-intensifies-exploration-of-gas-in-tripura-4769436/

26. *The Financial Express*. "India to Supply 500MW More to BD by July" (2017). Retrieved from https://bdnews24.com/economy/2017/10/26/india-to-supply-another-500mw-power-to-bangladesh-by-july-next-year.

27. Namgay, K. "Accelerating Hydropower Sector Development & Future Planning in Bhutan". *Nepal Power Investment Submit — 2016* (Kathmandu: Druk Green Power Corporation, 2016).

28. *India Hydro Energy*. Retrieved from EAI (2018). http://www.eai.in/ref/ae/hyd/hyd.html.

29. *Hydropower Status Report*. Beijing: International Hydropower Association (2018). Retrieved from India: https://www.hydropower.org/country-profiles/india

30. Priyantha Wijayatunga, D. C. *Cross-Border Power Trading in South Asia: A Techno Economic Rationale* (Manila: ADB, 2015).

31. Spot, E. *Epex Spot*. Retrieved from Epex Spot (2017). http://www.epexspot.com/en/company-info/about_epex_spot.29 *India Statistics*. Retrieved from International Hydropower Association (2017). https://www.hydropower.org/country-profiles.india.

32. Namgay, K. "Accelerating Hydropower Sector Development & Future Planning in Bhutan". *Nepal Power Investment Submit — 2016* (Kathmandu: Druk Green Power Corporation, 2016).

33. SARI/EI. *SARPEX*. Retrieved from SARI Energy (2017b). https://sari-energy.org/program-activities/regional-power-market/sarpex/.

Chapter 7

Climate and Energy Transition in South Asia: The Role of Regional Cooperation

Nitya Nanda

Introduction

The issue of climate change first entered the official regional discourse in the 14th SAARC Summit (New Delhi, April 3–4, 2007) as New Delhi Declaration called for pursuing a climate resilient development in South Asia. The 15th Summit meeting of the South Asian Association for Regional Cooperation (SAARC), held from August 2–3, 2008, in Colombo, Sri Lanka, concluded with the adoption of the Colombo Declaration entitled "Partnership for Growth for Our People", in which the Heads of State and Government reiterated the need for increased regional cooperation in tackling climate change, in particular for capacity building, the development of Clean Development Mechanism (CDM) projects, and awareness raising. Meanwhile, at the initiative of Bangladesh, an expert group meeting on climate change and a SAARC Ministerial Meeting of Climate Change were held. What came out of the process was a Regional Action Plan on Climate Change adopted in

July 2008 which emphasised coordinated regional actions in the following thematic areas:

- Adaptation to Climate Change
- Policies and Actions for Climate Change Mitigation
- Policies and Actions for Technology Transfer
- Finance and Investment
- Education and Awareness
- Management of impacts and risks due to climate Change
- Capacity building for international negotiations

Specific areas of action in the regional action plan for climate change for the region were to be identified according to the priorities outlined and actions envisaged in their own national action plans of the Member States. However, in April 2010, when the leaders of South Asia met during the 16th SAARC Summit, it was quite obvious that nothing has moved on the ground even two years after the adoption of the Regional Action Plan. Hence a special statement on climate change was issued which established a range of institutional mechanism to implement the regional action plan. Almost seven more years have passed since then, yet one wonders what has been achieved in terms of regional cooperation on climate change except a series of meetings.

The Context of Regional Cooperation on Climate Change

While the issue of capacity building for international negotiations was the last theme in the agenda of regional action plan on climate change in South Asia, this was actually the main issue that most countries in the region were grappling with. All other issues related to climate change took a backseat in the member countries of SAARC as the countries were deeply engaged with the UNFCCC process. While all South Asian countries have been a part of the G77 group that had a common position on climate negotiations at the UNFCCC, they had serious differences on some of the important issues.

The position of India, the dominant player in the region was often criticised by countries like Bangladesh and Nepal for its alleged "rigid position" that could have been responsible for holding up climate negotiations that could slow down the flow of climate funds to these countries. Maldives, which faces existential crisis due to climate change often accused India of indifference to the possible plight of countries like Maldives. India on the other hand thought that its neighbours failed to appreciate the complex position in which it has been *vis-à-vis* climate change, and its fight over larger issues like climate justice and equity, and instead have been under influence of developed countries. Interestingly, Pakistan, which generally did not share good relations with India, had often worked together with India on climate change issues.

The Paris Agreement, however, has drastically changed the context. Even the staunchest critiques of India's negotiating position during the pre-Paris Agreement days now concede that India showed huge courage to accept bold commitment to address the problem of climate change, probably beyond its means. India's INDC include reduction in the emissions intensity of its GDP by 33–35% by 2030 from the 2005 level and to create an additional carbon sink of 2.5–3 billion tonnes of CO_2 equivalent through additional forest and tree cover by 2030. India's INDC also builds on its goal of installing 175 GW of renewable power capacity (100 GW from solar alone) by 2022 by setting a new target to increase its share of non-fossil-based power capacity from 30% today to about 40% by 2030 (with the help of international support). Given this, increasing the share of non-fossil fuel from 30% today to 40% by 2030 does not seem to be ambitious. But nobody is complaining as the 2022 target is extremely ambitious, given that the world's entire installed solar power capacity was 181 GW in 2014, and it is unlikely that the 2022 target is going to be achieved. India has also given a positive signal to the global community by quickly ratifying the Paris Agreement.

A couple of other related developments are also important to consider in this context. The fifth assessment report of the Intergovernmental Panel on Climate Change (AR5 IPCC) published regional impacts from climate change which assessed that South Asia is one of the most vulnerable regions and the impacts are already being felt there. Changing patterns of rainfall and melting snow is impacting the freshwater system in the region. In future, climate change will impact flooding of human settlements, influence agricultural productivity, food and water scarcity, impacting both quantity and quality of available water in the region. Changes in temperature and monsoons will also impact the health and disease dynamics affecting not only human but animal population as well.

It is also noteworthy that the Paris Agreement also highlighted the need for regional cooperation to deal with the issues of climate change both from mitigation and adaptation perspectives. Environmental impacts do not follow national political boundaries. Just like there are issues that need global arrangement to be addressed effectively, there are issues that need to be handled at regional levels as well. This is more so in the context of adaptation. While the Paris Agreement has been hailed as a success, there has always been a measured sense of scepticism as well if it did enough to protect the climate. The rise of Donald Trump has put a further question mark on our ability to limit the rise of temperature below a target level. This means, adaptation to climate change is going to be even more important. The fact that South Asia, in many senses, represents an ecological system and hence regional cooperation becomes important to deal with the problem of climate change.

Impacts of climate change and the Paris Agreement on South Asia can be transmitted through several channels but they are not likely to be similar for all countries in the region as their climate concerns have been quite different. Impacts on different countries will be contingent upon their levels of commitments on one hand and their vulnerabilities to climate change on the other. At a broad level, the impacts will be felt mainly through the following two channels:

- Economic and social challenges that will arise from their mitigation commitments;
- Ability or inability of the Paris Agreement to limit the temperature rise below a specific level which will impact their burden of climate change adaptation.

Accordingly, regional cooperation on climate change can also happen in these two spheres. The following paragraphs briefly explore the possibilities of regional cooperation in South Asia in several areas of mitigation and adaptation.

Mitigation Commitments and Cooperation

Two countries in the region that have not made any unconditional mitigation commitment are Afghanistan and Pakistan. Pakistan intends to reduce up to 20% of its 2030 projected GHG emissions subject to availability of international grants to meet the total abatement cost which is estimated to be about US$40 billion (Pakistan INDC). Afghanistan intends to reduce its GHG emissions by 13.6% by 2030 compared to a business as usual 2030 scenario, entirely conditional on external support (Afghanistan INDC). In fact, Pakistan's lack of commitment has attracted criticism from domestic constituencies as well. Obviously, these two countries will not see any impacts from their mitigation commitments. All other countries have made both unconditional and conditional mitigation commitments.

While countries have made mitigation commitments that are spread across sectors, the core of it relates to the energy sector. Bangladesh pledged to reduce emission by 5% of 2030 BAU level unconditionally, which can go up to 15% if enough external support could be ensured (Bangladesh INDC). Bangladesh and India are facing a surging demand for energy on one hand and also dealing with the challenges of providing affordable and sustainable energy to their people. Given this, mitigation commitments of these two countries will severely restrict their choice in terms of meeting its fast growing demand for energy. This can also delay their efforts to ensure adequate and affordable energy for all in the near future.

Sri Lanka intends to reduce the GHG emissions against Business-As-Usual scenario unconditionally by 7% which might go up to 23% if enough additional resources were provided from external sources (Sri Lanka INDC). Similarly, Maldives committed to reduce 10% of its Greenhouse Gases (below BAU) for the year 2030 on its own, which can go up to 24% in the context of enough external support in terms of availability of financial resources, technology transfer and capacity building (Maldives INDC). While the unconditional commitments of these countries are quite modest, they are also relatively well placed in terms of access to energy and ability to meet current energy needs. Given this, they might not face much of the difficulties that might emerge from their mitigation commitments.

Nepal intends to reduce its dependency on fossil fuels by 50% and wants to generate 4,000 MW of hydroelectricity by 2020 and 12,000 MW by 2030. Additionally, it also wants to generate 2,100 MW of solar energy by 2030. Nepal's plan to equip every household in rural areas with smokeless (improved) cooking stoves by 2030 will not only add to mitigation but will bring substantial social benefits (Nepal INDC). The situation of Nepal is quite unique. Along with the low level of economic development, energy access scenario in the country is quite grim. It is also facing tremendous difficulty in meeting its current energy demand. It has made ambitious commitment to increase generation of hydroelectric power as well as solar and other forms of renewable energy. These targets will be difficult to meet but the difficulties will not come from commitment to reduce emissions. One unique feature of Nepal's commitment is providing affordable access to energy to its people, and hence if it achieves its targets, that will bring enormous socio-economic benefits to its people. Bhutan is a carbon neutral country and it will be quite easy for it to remain that way. The fact that it has huge hydropower potential, reasonably good energy access, huge forest cover and limited population will mean that it is in the most comfortable position to meet its mitigation commitments.

The current energy mix of South Asian countries are however quite different and hence their mitigation commitments will also have differential impacts. India is the only country that depends hugely on coal, particularly for electricity generation. Hence, India's commitment will involve both energy efficiency and more reliance on new and renewable energy. Bangladesh, where energy scenario is dominated by natural gas, there will be very little scope for reducing emission intensity by shifting to different fuels. Rather, the fact that it is facing shortage of natural gas will make it further difficult to reduce emission intensity as the country seems to be relying more on coal and coal-based electricity imported from India. While electricity generation in Nepal is mostly from hydropower, it imports nearly half of its electricity requirement from India which is coal-based. It will not be easy for Nepal to reduce its import dependence in the near future.

While, Sri Lanka has not used coal, its electricity generation uses oil in substantial quantity. With no infrastructure to import natural gas, its shift towards coal might not be ruled out. While Pakistan does not use coal now, and it plans to import natural gas as well as hydropower from Central Asia and also intends to import gas from Iran, in view of slow progress, it may also think of using lignite that it has in huge quantity. Afghanistan, of course, is likely to meet its growing demand from hydropower (Table 1).

Table 1:   Energy resources and potentials in South Asia.

Resources/Country	Bangladesh	Bhutan	India	Nepal	Afghanistan	Pakistan	Sri Lanka
Coal (Million MT)	293	—	56100	—		—	
Lignite (Million MT)	—	—	4500	1		2070	
Petroleum (Million MT)	3	—	740	—		—	
Natural Gas (Billion Cubic Metre)	200	—	1300	0		500	
Hydropower Potential (GW/year)	4000	263000	2638000	733000	55000	130000	8000
Hydro Generation (GW/Year)	1300	7134	114827	2759	250	31428	4552
Solar (GW Capacity)	—	—	657	—	222	230	7
Wind (GW Capacity)	—	—	49	3	67	50	20

Source: IEA Database and Nanda.[1]

The energy resource endowment of South Asian countries indicate that except India others do not have much of coal and hence they are unlikely to go for coal-based power generation in a major way. Regional trade and cooperation on energy in South Asia can help in several ways. It can help to deal with national level demand supply gaps as well as time of the day or seasonal fluctuations. It can also improve efficiency as there can be transmission rationalisation. A larger grid will be required for promotion of renewable energy. For example without integrating to India, Sri Lanka might find difficult to harness its wind power potentials. Generation of renewable energy for cross-border use can also be an option for boosting energy supplies in the region and at the same time can keep combined emission of the region at a relatively lower level. For example, solar energy from Pakistan can go to India, solar energy from UP, Bihar (of India) can go to Nepal, solar energy in Tripura can go to Bangladesh; wind energy from Sri Lanka can go to India.

Elusive cooperation in natural gas

Natural gas can play an important role in fulfilling mitigation commitments of South Asian countries. However, except India, and more recently Pakistan, nobody in SA engages in the natural gas trade as there is no infrastructure. For India, access to assured gas supplies continues to be uncertain and India frequently pays higher prices for spot LNG purchases. Though gas use for electricity generation in India is not very high, still it is the third largest source of electricity after coal and hydropower. For Bangladesh, natural gas has been the mainstay of electricity generation and there was a time when it was thought that Bangladesh had substantial surplus of natural gas. Hence, the first proposal to export natural gas from Bangladesh to India came from one of the foreign producers operating in Bangladesh. Unocal (now Chevron) which had developed a gasfield in north-eastern Bangladesh proposed the construction of an 847 mile (1,363 km) gas pipeline from Bibiyana to New Delhi.[2] However, the issue became politically contentious in Bangladesh and the proposal was nipped in the bud. With natural gas being the only energy resource available in the country, it was quite reluctant to export gas. By now it is quite clear that Bangladesh cannot export natural gas or gas-based electricity even in future. However, gas-based cooperation between these two countries is still possible. An important factor in India–Bangladesh cooperation in the field of natural gas could be Myanmar which has estimated natural gas reserves of 89.722 tcf, of which 18.012 tcf are considered proven recoverable reserves.

In order to transport this gas to India, negotiations were held with the Bangladesh government to provide transit facilities from time to time. Although in January 2005, Bangladesh agreed to allow the 559 mile pipeline to pass through its territory yet such acceptance by the Bangladesh government, was subject to several conditions including grant of several trade concessions including removal of tariff, non-tariff and administrative barriers to Bangladesh exports to India, provision of access to hydroelectricity from Nepal and Bhutan and an establishment of the free trade corridor to these countries.[3] India, at that point of time, was not willing to give these concessions to Bangladesh but by now has agreed to all these demands made by Bangladesh. However, the gas pipeline is not in place. The reticence in decision-making cost India, and Myanmar decided to sell the available gas to China. The construction of the Myanmar–China pipeline project which consists of dual oil and gas pipelines originating at Kyaukpyu port on the west coast of Myanmar and entering China at Yunnan's border city of Ruili also worked in favour of China.

However, such a hard bargain cost Bangladesh as well. By now, the energy situation has changed significantly in Bangladesh. It has started facing shortage of gas, mainly due to its inability to tap full potential as well as failure to find significant additional reserves. Hence Bangladesh also toyed with the idea of importing gas from Myanmar. Realising that a Myanmar Bangladesh pipeline was not economically viable, in 2010, the Bangladesh government has finally given its approval of a potential Myanmar–Bangladesh–India pipeline.[4] The lack of convergence in the energy policies of India and Bangladesh cost both the countries. The discovery of the offshore North–West Myanmar Gas Field — estimated to contain reserves of between 120 and 170 billion cubic metres of gas — has sparked new hope and renewed interest in the proposed Pipeline.

Pakistan, till recently, did not have any infrastructure to import gas. There is a proposal to extend to Lahore a natural gas pipeline India has recently installed from the west coast to Bhatinda in Indian Punjab which is around

25-km away from the India–Pakistan border. Imported LNG can move through the Dahej–Vijaipur–Dadri–Bawana–Nangal–Bhatinda pipeline and then into Pakistan. Pakistan is experiencing its worst gas crisis. Pakistan has a couple of LNG import terminals but the capacity is inadequate to meet its needs. Building of additional capacity will take some time, while the existing pipeline in India can be extended to Lahore within months.

It needs to be noted that natural gas is the energy for transition for several uses. Major international gas pipelines have been planned for the region but without any success. The first to be mooted was the Iran–Pakistan–India (IPI) pipeline proposed by TERI in 1989. Turkmenistan–Afghanistan–Pakistan–India (TAPI) was conceptualised as TAP in 1995 and India proposed to join in 2008. Now it is proposed to be completed by 2020. India was also quite keen on the Myanmar–Bangladesh–India (MBI) pipeline but could not make any progress due to bilateral differences. Even IPI could not progress due to bilateral differences over transit fees but security concerns are also believed to be the reasons. MBI is a missed opportunity. Pakistan went ahead with IP but could not progress due to lack of funding. Iran is interested in the Iran–Pakistan–India–Bangladesh (IPIB) pipeline as well. A regional approach might help. If such pipeline network is used also to serve Nepal and Bhutan's needs for natural gas that can help in addressing Indian apprehensions on security challenges.

Electricity cooperation

While regional cooperation on electricity is still a far cry, there has been substantial progress involving India and some of its neighbours. India–Bhutan cooperation is a success story and it made significant impact on Bhutan's GDP, Export, Revenue and Human Development. Electricity accounts for about 20% of GDP, one-third of government revenue and nearly half of exports. The first project with Indian collaboration, Chukha Hydropower Plant started in 1978 and fully commissioned in 1988. Hydropower projects in Bhutan were built mainly with Indian financial assistance with a significant grant component and technical assistance as well. Bhutan has plans to increase up to 10,000 MW with an Indian guarantee to purchase half of it. It can be replicated in countries like Nepal, but not on a scale that can make similar impacts in Nepal. Moreover, so far, the Bhutan story is more about political and diplomatic success and is not market-based.

As far as India–Nepal cooperation is concerned, existing linkage is minimal. Several projects are in the pipelines but with not much progress. It has a long history of cooperation and some unfulfilled expectations. Once Nepal was keen but India was not, then India changed its position but the situation changed in Nepal. There are political differences as well as opposition from CSOs. Private companies from India (Sutlej/GMR) are interested but the government is slow in action. There is stiff opposition in Nepal due to potential environmental and social implications, but the cost of non-cooperation in Nepal is also quite high. Nepal faces severe power shortage, and also has the second lowest energy access in South Asia only after Afghanistan. Import of electricity, diesel, and kerosene causes severe stress on BoP which also increases indebtedness. Excessive use of diesel and kerosene also causes related environmental/social challenges. Excessive use of woods also has social and environmental implications including massive deforestation, soil erosion and land degradation. Bhutan, on the other hand, is a carbon neutral country that protects its forests, apart from its much better health and education indicators.

More recently, there has been substantial progress on energy cooperation between Bangladesh and India. As of now, about 600 MW of electricity is flowing through Berhampore–Bheramara transmission line on the western side of Bangladesh and Suryamani Nagar–Comilla transmission line on the eastern side. While the full transmission capacity is being utilised in the western sector, an additional 300 MW of power can be transmitted in the eastern sector. Moreover, transmission capacity on the western side is also being enhanced.

India is developing several hydropower projects in the north-eastern states. Once these plants become operational, it will lead to a situation when supply of power in this region will far outweigh demand in the region. If the surplus power needs to be transmitted to other regions of India through the narrow stretch of Siliguri corridor in West Bengal, it will face some obstacles. India intends to evacuate this surplus power through the Bangladesh territory. Part of the power can be consumed in Bangladesh as well. However, there has not been any concrete progress in this regard.

Like in other sectors, energy cooperation between India and Pakistan has been elusive. In 1998, India proposed to import power from Pakistan but this was not implemented due to pricing issues (India offered 2.2 cents (US)/unit while Pakistan demanded 7.2 cents). In the changed situation, Pakistan could be interested to import from India (initially 500 MW). Pakistan's 500 KV transmission system extends from Jamshoro in the south to Tarbela and Peshawar in the north. These lines run very near to the adjoining borders of India Dinanath (Lahore) in Pakistan and Patti (Amritsar) in India are designated substations.[5]

While India is making progress towards renewable energy, the same can create a situation that might have implications for mitigation commitments of neighbouring countries that are linked to the Indian grid. India already has a surplus in electricity which is predominantly coal-based. However, creation of solar capacity would also mean that it will still need coal-based power to deal with its peak-demand that occurs at night when solar power is not available. This is likely as solar capacity is going up but no progress is seen in the creation of storage capacity. Once capacity is created, solar power capacity can be offered at very low cost if the market is competitive as the variable cost of solar power generation is very low. Hence, even coal-based power will be sold at lower prices particularly during day time. This development might push countries like Bangladesh and Nepal to import more of coal-based power from India. Even Pakistan which is suffering huge electricity shortage might look towards India for import of coal-based power from India.

To boost electricity demand as well as reducing emission intensity of the transport sector and reduce local pollution, India is emphasising on the electrification of its transport sector. While this will not reduce emission intensity of the transportation as long as the electric grid remains coal dependent, it will make the transport sector ready for emission reduction as and when the grid is able to reduce its coal dependence. However, in the short run, this might make India's peak demand even higher, which in the absence of storage capacity will make India's coal-based power even more attractive to neighbouring countries.

One common challenge that almost all South Asian countries face is the issue of black carbon. While the major source of black carbon is the use of traditional fuel like biomass for household cooking, brick kiln and crop residue burning are other major sources. In fact, crop residue burning has become a major factor that has raised air pollution to hazardous levels in several cities in India and Pakistan including Delhi and Lahore. While households need cleaner cooking fuel for maintaining cleaner air at homes, it is quite impossible for them to reduce their reliance on biomass. It is therefore important that these countries look for cleaner technologies for using biomass for cooking. Similar technological solutions will be required for brick kiln and crop residue burning including possible use of crop residue and alternative building materials.

BBIN energy corridor and engaging with ASEAN countries

In view of the lack of progress in South Asia wide energy cooperation and trade, promoting such cooperation at subregional level involving Bangladesh, Bhutan, India and Nepal (BBIN) could become a reality in the near future as the countries involved seem to be willing. India was earlier reluctant to transmit power from Nepal and Bhutan to Bangladesh through Indian territory but now supports it enthusiastically. Neither Bhutan, nor Nepal has any hydrocarbon reserves. Globally, most countries are switching from oil to gas on both economic and environmental grounds. However, Bhutan and Nepal have not been able to initiate the process as they do not have access to natural gas. Hence, cooperation on natural gas through pipelines can be an important component of BBIN cooperation initiative which can substantially reduce polluting petroleum oil in the transport sector in these countries, particularly in Nepal and Bhutan where this sector constitutes the major source of emission.

BBIN energy cooperation could become more meaningful if Myanmar is also brought into this framework. While Bangladesh–India energy cooperation in the context of accessing natural gas from Myanmar has been discussed for quite some time, there is now a possibility that it could take a broader form. ASEAN has been an energy-surplus region, yet its surplus energy has generally moved eastward rather than westward. Against this backdrop, it will be interesting to explore if the energy-thirsty South Asia, BBIN in particular, and the resource-rich ASEAN can promote wider cooperation on energy security that can be mutually beneficial to both the regions.

ASEAN is in the process of developing a region wide grid of natural gas pipelines and electricity transmission lines. BBIN can get connected to these two ASEAN wide grids just by developing transmission line and gas pipeline connections with Myanmar. In the future, it may be possible for Bangladesh and India not only to access electricity and gas from Myanmar but also gas from faraway fields in Indonesia and Brunei and electricity from Lao PDR.

While India–ASEAN energy cooperation focuses on renewable energy only, India, along with Bangladesh, Bhutan, Nepal and some members of ASEAN, are part of the Bay of Bengal Initiative for Multi-Sectoral Technical and Economic Cooperation (BIMSTEC), where energy has been identified as one of the important sectors for cooperation. BIMSTEC can thus, work as a bridge between BBIN and ASEAN in promoting a comprehensive energy cooperation regime. India is already engaged in energy infrastructure development in the ASEAN region particularly in the Cambodia, Lao PDR, Myanmar and Vietnam (CLMV) countries. India is building hydropower projects, power transmission lines and substations and oil and gas pipelines in these countries.

Adaptation Requirements and Regional Cooperation

As noted before, the effectiveness of the Paris Agreement to address the challenge of climate change has always been a concern and the ascendance of Donald Trump to the US Presidency has added to the concern. In this context, all South Asian countries are on the same boat. While it may be imagined that different countries will have differential impacts, they might be more of notions and perspectives. While Maldives might be facing an existential crisis, the sheer enormity of the problem in India makes it no less of a challenge. India has a long coastline and huge stretches of low lying areas, a large part of the country is suffering from water stress. It has a huge stretch of ecologically fragile mountainous areas and a huge population that is going to reach the 1.5 billion mark whose food and health security will need to be ensured in the context of climate change. Half of Bangladesh is in low lying areas and faces the threat of inundation due to climate change; it is already a country that is a victim of extreme weather events and disasters.

Much of Sri Lanka is either coastal and low-lying areas highly susceptible to extreme weather events like storm surge, or ecologically fragile mountainous areas. Hence, the entire country is highly vulnerable to climate change. Vulnerability of Afghanistan is not only very high in terms of potential impacts of climate change; extreme poverty makes its people even more vulnerable. Pakistan is the most water-stressed country in the region and it is already feeling the impacts of climate change in agriculture. Hence maintaining food security could be huge challenge for the country. Nepal is an ecologically fragile mountainous country with high probability of impending climate-related disasters. It already suffers from a fragile food security situation and widespread poverty among its people. While the mitigation scenario looks good for Bhutan, the entire country is ecologically sensitive and extremely vulnerable to climate-related disasters.

Costs of mitigation that South Asian countries have committed, particularly, that of conditional type, is likely to be quite high. Most countries of South Asia have not yet been able to make an assessment of their mitigation and adaptation costs. Moreover, while some countries have made some assessment of mitigation costs, they have been unable to make any comprehensive assessment of adaptation costs. This is because while a country can make a mitigation plan, adaptation needs will remain uncertain. At best, some countries have made some sector-specific or activity-based assessment of adaptation costs. Nevertheless, it is well recognised that the costs of adaptation in South Asia as whole is likely to be huge and the countries will find it extremely hard to mobilise the necessary resources from domestic sources.

Afghanistan has suggested a financial need of about US$17.405 billion (2020–2030), of which US$10.785 billion is for adaptation and US$6.62 billion is for mitigation (Afghanistan INDC). Pakistan has indicated a figure of about US$40 billion (at current prices) for mitigation and an amount ranging between U$7 and 14 billion per annum for adaptation (Pakistan INDC). Bangladesh has indicated that adaptation needs related to some sectors and activities will cross US$40 billion (Bangladesh INDC).

According to some estimates, India is already spending about US$100 billion a year for adaption which is likely to reach US$360 billion a year by the year 2030.[6] According to another estimate, India's emission intensity-reduction targets and adaptation to climate change will require about US$2.5 trillion by the year 2030, as well as an array of technologies (India INDC). According to one estimate, costs of adaptation in Nepal agriculture could be about US$20,000 per villages excluding the costs that might be incurred at the national or district levels.[7]

According to a 2014 study conducted by the Asian Development Bank, in a BAU scenario, South Asia could lose an equivalent of 1.8% of its annual gross domestic product (GDP) by 2050, which will progressively increase to 8.8% by 2100. It also suggests that even if the temperature rise can be contained within two degree Celsius, the region would lose an average of 1.3% of GDP by 2050 and roughly 2.5% by 2100. According to the study, the Maldives will be the hardest hit with a 2.3% loss in GDP, while Bangladesh, Bhutan, India, Nepal and Sri Lanka are respectively projected to face 2.0%, 1.4%,1.8%, 2.2% and 1.2% loss of annual GDP by 2050.[8] While it needs to be recognised that monetary costs of climate change is only a small part of the total costs as they will not adequately capture the suffering of the people, when we make an assessment of adaptation costs, particularly in relation to needs for external assistance of these countries, these are important to consider.

It is quite unlikely that South Asian countries are going to get the kind of external assistance they are looking for. Countries like Afghanistan, Maldives, Sri Lanka and Bhutan can get a sizeable proportion of the costs for adaptation and mitigation from external finance. But for countries like India, Bangladesh, Pakistan and Nepal, the external assistance they might get is likely to be miniscule compared to their overall needs despite the fact that Bangladesh and Nepal have the status of least developed countries. Furthermore, much of the mitigation commitment of developing countries are conditional and hence failure to generate enough finance for them will mean further deviation from mitigation targets leading to greater needs for adaptation.

In view of the discussion above, it is quite obvious that South Asian countries are likely to face enormous adaptation challenges and they have to fend for themselves without much external assistance. While they must try to fulfil their mitigation commitments, there is huge scope for regional cooperation on adaptation challenges. It is thus important to highlight some key areas of adaptation that South Asian countries can work together on.

Water resources

The South Asian countries are home to about one-fourth of the world's population, but contain only about 4.5% (1,945 billion m³) of the world's annual renewable water resources (43,659 billion m³). The Hindu Kush–Himalayan region (HKH) is amongst the largest storehouses of fresh water in the world which constitute the primary source of water for about 700 million people in South Asia. While some parts of India and Bangladesh are already in stress, in Pakistan, the overall withdrawal of fresh water is already more than what is sustainable. This is largely due to overexploitation of groundwater. Fresh water utilisation level is more than 15% in the GBM basin but it is more than 90% in the Indus basin. While the region gets significant rainfalls, there are wide spatial and temporal variations. Because of this, countries in the region depend heavily on ground water. Overexploitation of groundwater can reduce flows in the rivers in the lean seasons, which affects the lower riparian regions in many ways.

Deforestation and degradation of forests along with climate change have been blamed for increased frequency of cloud bursts in the Himalayan regions. Such events cause problems not only in the hills but in the plains below through floods and sudden release of excessive sediments triggered by landslides. While the Himalayan rivers have historically caused floods and brought down sediments, what has changed is the frequency and intensity of such events.

The GBM delta is the home of the famous Sundarbans with its unique ecosystem. The existence of Sundarbans and its flora and fauna are threatened not only by possible sea level rise but also by what happens to the flow of the GBM rivers that have created this, apart from urbanisation and aquaculture.

The salinity balance of the oceans plays an important role in the complex interactions between atmosphere and sea that determines climate and monsoon over the South Asian region. In particular, the Bay of Bengal gets huge discharge of freshwater from several mighty rivers including

GBM, Mahanadi, Godavari, Krishna and Kaveri from South Asia and also from Irrawaddy in Myanmar. As a result, the salinity level of surface water in the Bay is low. This low-salinity surface water allows the Bay to remain warm and sustain cloud systems. While the recent increase in frequency in storm surges in the region is often attributed to climate change, it is also important to consider the issue of change in salinity balance that might have been occurring. Moreover, this low salinity level along with the total organic carbon deposited by these rivers has created a unique marine ecology in the Bay, which also has the world's largest submarine fan. This has made the bay a bio-diversity hotspot. Lack of adequate flow or any change in the flow pattern can seriously harm this marine biodiversity.

It is quite obvious that these challenges cannot be addressed by a single country. The need for basin wide management of river basins cutting across political boundaries is accepted in principle but hardly implemented in practice, particularly in South Asia.

Agriculture and food security

Food security has been one of the major challenges that the region has been facing. To deal with such challenges, countries have made significant technological interventions, much of which has been imported rather than indigenously developed. Such technologies have also created problems adding stress to the long-run sustainability of the agricultural sector itself. Hence, it is important that South Asian countries come together to deal with impacts of climate change in agriculture that are already being felt or likely to be felt in the near future. There are existing technologies, methods and practices that can be useful in addressing adaptation challenges in other parts of the region as well. There is also a huge scope for pooling of research and technological capabilities that can bring better R&D outcomes that will help climate change adaptation in the region.

Disaster management

It is well acknowledged that the region is likely to face more extreme weather events in the future, necessitating greater needs for disaster management activities. An important aspect of natural disaster is that not the entire region is going to be hit by some disaster at any point of time. For a small country, however, a disaster may completely paralyse the response capacity and it will need help from others to deal with the challenges. South Asian countries have been helping each other, but more on an ad hoc basis. There has also been some institutionalised response to promote cooperation on disaster management but it needs substantial strengthening.

Health impacts

Just like agriculture, health is another area that will be badly hit due to impacts of climate change. The existing diseases might spread further or might be felt with higher intensity with greater health impacts. New diseases might also come into the picture. Since people of different countries share similar biological profiles, there is the likelihood that climate change might create similar health impacts. Hence there is a case for taking up collaborative health research. There is also the possibility that the health research taken up in other parts of the world might bypass the health needs of the South Asian population and hence regional R&D efforts can be useful, which can also bring optimum outcomes.

Conclusion

While the Paris Agreement has imposed only modest pressure on South Asian countries in terms of mitigation costs, the fact that the Agreement is not strong enough is likely to leave South Asia with a huge adaptation burden. South Asian countries are also unlikely to get access to enough of external resources to deal with climate change-related challenges. Given this, there is a greater need for the countries to work together. Regional energy cooperation would help develop renewable energy not only in India but other countries as well. Though the region has been discussing such cooperation for a long time, little has been achieved on the ground. One way to stimulate change would be to start a few climate-related projects under the SAARC Development Fund by expanding its mandate.

End Notes

1. Nanda, Nitya. "Energy Market Integration and Cooperation", in RIS (Ed.), *ASEAN-India Development and Cooperation Report 2015* (New Delhi: Routledge, 2015).
2. Bose, Srinjoy. *Energy Politics: India-Bangladesh-Myanmar Relations*. IPCS Special Report, No. 45 (New Delhi: Institute of Peace and Conflict Studies, 2007).
3. World Bank, Sustainable Development Department, South Asia Region (2007), Potential and Prospects for Regional Energy Trade in the South Asia Region, New Delhi.
4. Chandra, Varigonda Kesava. 'The Pipeline That Wasn't: Myanmar–Bangladesh–India Natural Gas Pipeline". *Journal of Energy Security* (2012).
5. Lama, Mahendra P. "India-Pakistan Energy Cooperation: Rethinking Opportunities and Newer Approaches", in Nisha Taneja and Sanjib Pohit (Eds.), *India–Pakistan Trade: Strengthening Economic Relations* (New York: Springer, 2015), pp. 311–315.
6. CEEW. *Getting a Deal: CEEW Climate Research, Engagements and Contributions to COP21 Negotiations* (New Delhi: CEEW, 2016).
7. IIED. *Costing Agriculture's Adaptation to Climate Change.* IIED Briefing Paper (2011).
8. Ahmed, M. and S. Suphachalasai. *Assessing the Costs of Climate Change and Adaptation in South Asia* (Mandaluyong City, Philippines: Asian Development Bank, 2014).

Section 2
India

Chapter 8

Transitioning Towards a Sustainable Energy Future: Challenges and Opportunities for India*

Vikram Singh Mehta

Introduction

New Delhi in India has become the most polluted city in the world.[1] In New Delhi, one can smell the noxious fumes emitted by the burning of harvest stubble and vehicular traffic and one feels surrounded by the sight and noise of a construction site. A visit to New Delhi would persuade even the most hardened environmental sceptic that the present model of economic development is unsustainable; that the growing chorus of concern about climate change is not a scientific hoax; and that the world simply does not have the luxury of staying on the treadmill of high carbon growth.

*This paper is an adaptation of the keynote address delivered at the ISAS-ESI Conference on "Towards a Low Carbon Asia: The Challenges of Ensuring Efficient and Sustainable Energy", on November 28, 2017. The conference was organised by the Institute of South Asian Studies (ISAS), an autonomous research institute at the National University of Singapore (NUS), in partnership with the Energy Security Institute (ESI), also from NUS.

Therefore, the organisers of this conference must be commended on the framing of the topic because it recognises this urgency. It compels reflection on the "how", not as is all too often the case, on the "why" or the "what". Much of the discussion and analysis, so far, has focused on the reasons for and the shape of the current crisis. There is also a library of literature on what needs to be done to adapt to and mitigate the consequential impact. Not enough work has been done, however, on how to implement the identified solutions. This conference focused on "how" and, in particular, the modalities of moving forward down the pathway towards a low carbon future, and thus, an attempt to correct this imbalance.

India sits at the nub of the crisis of the current high carbon model of development. It is not responsible for this crisis and it can legitimately argue that it must not bear the costs of adapting and mitigating its consequences. However, it cannot escape the reality that it is amongst the most vulnerable nations to global warming. This paper identifies five factors that define the reality of India's energy sector and argues that these factors should be regarded as predetermined trends that will influence the shape of India's future energy profile, at least for the foreseeable future, irrespective of the specifics of policy. It underlines that the Indian government recognises the severity of the problem and has embarked on an ambitious programme to tackle the crisis on its own. However, it requires better alignment of the political, institutional and financial framework for implementation in a given time-frame. Further, the paper lays out five propositions that are necessary first steps towards a low carbon future.

Global Consensus on the Way Forward

The scientific and physical evidence regarding global warming is overwhelming. Temperature change is not a recent phenomenon. It has been a characteristic of our ecosystem for a millennia. What is different today is that the pace of change, and the fact that the natural ecosystem is not able to accommodate to this pace. Human activity has disrupted the balance. United States (US) President Donald Trump may question the causality but he will be hard pressed to dismiss the empirical and physical evidence. Global mean temperatures are today approximately 1.5 degrees higher than in pre-industrial times and the concentration of Greenhouse Gas

(GHG) in the atmosphere is fast moving to the tipping point of 450 parts per million, beyond which, our planet will face severe and possibly irremediable consequences.[2]

The global community has now acknowledged this reality. The Paris accord[3] is a testament of this recognition. The accord does not commit the signatories to actions that will contain the increase in global temperatures to below 2 degrees Centigrade relative to the temperature prevailing in the pre-industrial era — the level beyond which the scientific community believes the ecological system will be structurally imbalanced — but it does establish that the world is aligned on the objective of low carbon development. The Paris accord also establishes that, whilst its signatories continue to differ over details, for instance, the treatment of carbon, the optimal mix between risk and reward, the financing mechanism and, in particular, the paymaster, that is, who should pick up the tab, they agree on the steps that must be tread to achieve this objective.

The world must move away from a fossil fuel-based energy system — it must enhance the share of renewables in the energy basket; it should improve the efficiency of energy usage and encourage demand conservation; the protection of forests and reforestation must be a policy priority and greater resources should be allocated for research and development (R&D) of clean energy technologies.

What the Paris accord could not achieve was alignment on the political, institutional and financial framework required for implementation of these measures, and the time frame. This was a lacuna, for, as history teaches us, we cannot assume that technology is panacea for all our problems. We may have the technological answers to a problem but there is a long lag between the development of those answers and their full impact on systems, processes and our way of life.

Historical Caveat

Information technology may have made us complacent, for its impact has been immediate and dramatic. It has revolutionised our lives within a generation. History, however, offers an opposite and somewhat salutary lesson. It tells us that the full impact of new technology depends on a slew of complimentary investments in infrastructure, structures, organisation and training.

These investments are often delayed and, consequently, there is a long lag between the development of new technology and its impact on society.

Two economists from Dartmouth University, Diego Colin and Bart Hobijn, provide empirical confirmation of this historical trend. They surveyed the application of 15 technologies across 166 countries and concluded that, on average, countries adopted technologies 45 years after their invention.[4] More specifically, Edison illuminated the lower half of Manhattan in 1885. However, it was not until the mid-1930s that all the factories in the US had converted from steam power to electric power. This was because they were not structured for this revolutionary new technology. Most had to be redesigned; some had to be rebuilt.

The larger point is that the "the clean energy" technologies required to shift away from a fossil fuel-based energy system towards a low carbon energy system are known to us and they are fast approaching the threshold of commerciality and competitiveness against incumbent "fossil fuel" technologies. There is good reason, therefore, to be optimistic about the pace at which solar and wind can replace oil, gas and coal for electricity generation and industrial processes. India has, for instance, targeted an exponential growth of solar electricity from the current approximate of 15 GW to around 100 GW by 2022. However, this optimism must be tempered. History is signalling caution. It is forewarning that, in the absence of these associated investments coupled with statesmanship and political will, the clean energy option will only appeal to a small, specialised section of the country. The historical cue is that it is one thing to have the technological answers; it is another to scale its application and effect a systemic change.

India: Epicentre of Global Warming

India presently finds itself at the crux of the high carbon model of development — a crisis for which it is not responsible. As such, it can rightly argue against bearing any cost to deal with its ramifications.

However, it cannot escape the reality that it is amongst the most vulnerable nations to global warming. Two-thirds of its population are agriculturalists dependent on the monsoons for their livelihood. They would be hugely impacted by climate change-induced unseasonality in rainfall. Another 150 million or so live alongside its 7,000-km coastline. They would face the consequences of climate change rise in the mean sea level. Its northern perimeter is fringed with approximately 10,000 Himalayan glaciers. Scientists have observed an alarming increase in the rate of retreat of these glaciers. The evidence is mixed but most people agree that climate change is, most likely, a contributory cause. What is indubitable is the fact that glacial recession will worsen the cycle of flooding and drought that currently afflicts large parts of North India every year.

The Indian government recognises the severity of the problem. It also realises that it does not have the luxury to wait upon the actions of the global community. It needs to tackle the crisis on its own. So, towards this end, it has embarked on an ambitious, some might say audacious, programme of development of solar, wind and bio energy; it has publicly committed its intent to increase the share of renewables in electricity generation to 40% by 2030; to reduce the emissions of GHG by between 30–35% relative to 2005 by 2035 and to shift the production of new cars to electric vehicles (EVs) by 2030. This is a laudable programme.

The question is whether it is feasible or indeed advisable. Some, including the Indian government's Chief Economic Adviser Arvind Subramanian, are suggesting that it is not feasible or advisable. While the later part of this paper touches upon his reasons for caution, it is important to stress that the feasibility of such an ambitious programme will depend on timely investments in the associated and complimentary infrastructure. And for that, pragmatic answers will have to be found to questions such as:

- How does one remove the roadblocks to the development of smart infrastructure, smart cities and smart buildings?
- What needs to be done to accelerate the implementation of energy-efficient technologies?
- What new financial instruments must be created to raise the required capital? and
- What organisational and institutional changes must accompany these efforts?

The answers to these questions must be framed within the existing socio-economic and political realities of the energy sector for a greater practical value.

India: Framework for Implementation

Five factors define the reality of India's energy sector. These should be regarded as predetermined trends that will influence the shape of India's future energy profile, at least for the foreseeable future, irrespective of the specifics of policy.

The first is the fact that energy is a concurrent subject under the Indian constitution. This means that the Central government, the 29 State governments and six Union territories have concurrent legislative competence and authority for administrative action. The consequence of this overlap of roles and responsibilities has been the creation of a fragmented energy market. India does not have a single unified market for energy. This is exemplified by the tariff structure for electric power. There are today, nearly 100 varying tariffs. A religious establishment pays a different tariff than a bus station; a farmer with irrigable land is charged a higher tariff than a farmer dependent on the monsoons; a breeder of rabbits is treated differently than one who keeps poultry. This extraordinary potpourri reflects the competing tugs and pulls of competitive federalism, populist politics and the influence of vested stakeholders. Therefore, a systemic shift of radical dimensions will be required to simplify, straitjacket and unify the energy market.

The second is the fact that the natural resource base for energy is unevenly spread in terms of endowment, geography, investment and structure. India has the fifth largest deposits of coal in the world. The bulk of these deposits are, however, located in the North and East of India whereas the principal consumption centres are in the West and South of the country. Further, the coal industry is effectively controlled by the Indian government through the state-owned monolith, "Coal India".

In contrast, India is not comparably well endowed with oil. It produces barely 20% of its requirements and imports the balance 80% from predominantly the Middle East, Nigeria and Venezuela through principally the deep water ports of Mumbai, Jamnagar and Hazera. Unlike coal, the oil industry has been liberalised and whilst the oil and gas value chain is dominated by state-owned entities — Oil and Natural Gas commission in the upstream, and Indian Oil Company, Bharat Petroleum Company and Hindustan Petroleum Company in the downstream. The private sector has a presence (and, in the case of refining, the dominant presence) and the operating and commercial conditions are aligned to the market.

Regarding renewables, although these contribute a minuscule share of India's energy requirement, it is worth noting that the investments in solar and wind have been skewed towards a handful of States. Eight of the country's 29 States attract the entirety of the investment. This is, in part, because of weather patterns and, in part, because of specific State government incentives. The private sector is the lead player but the economics of the business depends almost totally on government largesse.

This uneven spread of resources, policy, structure and investment has created vested political, social and economic linkages that militate against change. The coal industry exemplifies this reality. "Coal India" is choked by strong labour unions, the Mafioso and cronyism. It is subject to the vagaries of the road and railway transport infrastructure. It confronts, in short, the tugs and pulls of several competing stakeholders. The most effective way of managing these pressures is by subserving the status quo. This systemic reality is not unique to the coal industry. It afflicts the entire energy industry.

The third is the fact that fossil fuels and coal, in particular, will remain the backbone of India's energy system for the foreseeable future. The government think tank the National Institution for Transforming India (NITI Aayog) has projected that coal, oil and gas will account for 77% of the country's energy system in 2040. Their projection is not intended to call into question the government's commitment to develop renewables. It is simply to acknowledge an economic and political reality. Coal is the cheapest and most abundant source of energy, and politicians and the government need to meet their commitment to provide every citizen access to affordable and reliable electricity. Hence, India faces a conundrum.

How does India square the circle between, on one hand, its commitment to reduce GHG emissions and, on the other, its investment in the "dirtiest" of fuels? There is no easy way to crack this issue. The Chief Economic Adviser has suggested that India simply accept that, whilst renewables are an important offset against global warming and environmental degradation, the time has not yet arrived for the government to put its eggs into the renewables basket. His argument is grounded on solid economics. Solar and wind are not competitive against coal and they will not be so for years, notwithstanding Swanson's law that the cost of solar photovoltaic panels will drop by 20% for every doubling of cumulative shipped volumes — that is, at the present rates of production, the costs will halve every 10 years — and notwithstanding, the inclusion of a carbon charge. He has forewarned the government against the "double whammy" implications of pushing renewables for two reasons. First, it will increase the subsidy bill because renewables are not sustainable without subsidies. And, second, it will strand existing thermal power plants. The plant load factor (PLF) of thermal power plants has been trending downwards for some time and a surge in renewable energy capacity could well push the PLF below the threshold of viability of approximately 50%. Dr Subramanian has invoked St Augustine to summarise his approach to renewable, "Lord give me continence and chastity but not yet". One may challenge the assumptions that underpin his conclusions and one may counter St Augustine with a paraphrase of Blaise Pascal's famous remark regards divinity — the price of denying the existence of God could be an eternity in hell if one was wrong (about global warming) — but that still does not take away from the prevailing reality. Coal will remain the bulwark of our energy system for the foreseeable future because of "good politics".

The fourth is the fact of surging demand. India has a huge population; a rising percentage of this population are migrant and aspirational. They are moving from rural to urban India and they are looking to trade up, metaphorically speaking, from a cycle to a motorised two wheeler to eventually a car. Moreover, its economy has now entered its most energy-intensive phase of development with the "Make in India" manufacturing, the centrepiece of government policy. Finally, there is the "consumption-inducing" impact of subsidies. Petroleum products (liquid petroleum gas, LPG, kerosene and diesel) have been subsidised for years. This has distorted the market and led to what people have often referred to as the "dieselisation" of the economy. This government has taken advantage of the fall in international oil prices to lower the level of subsidies and rationalise the price structure. This has corrected somewhat the distortions but not fully. LPG and kerosene continue to be subsidised. Population, prosperity and policy explain the historic surge in demand.

One should presume that all three factors will remain in play and the demand for petroleum products will continue to ratchet upwards.

The fifth and final is the fact that energy sits at the core of every politician's deepest dilemma. Democratically-elected leaders have to reconcile the calculus of 'good economics' with the pressures of "good politics". They often know what needs to be done. What they do not know is how to get re-elected thereafter! This is why, all too often, they push "good economics" to the side. New Delhi is today blanketed by the smoke caused by the burning of the residue of the recent harvest by farmers in the neighbouring States of Haryana, Punjab and Rajasthan. Every year, the farmers burn the residue to prepare their field for the next sowing cycle. And every year, the wind blows the smoke across to New Delhi. Good environmental economics would have prompted the governments of the four States (New Delhi is also a State) to provide the farmers with the equipment required to prevent the burning. The cost is inconsequential relative to the cost of air pollution. However, that has not happened because of competitive politics. And so, every year, New Delhi and its surrounding areas choke under a deathly blanket of smog.

Ultimately, the effectiveness of any "low carbon" programme will rest on striking the right balance between economic logic, political compulsion and environmental imperative. The dilemma will, however, persist.

The Way Forward: Five Propositions

This section lays out five propositions that fit within the above framework and are necessary first steps towards a low carbon future. The hope is that, in taking these first few steps, the platform will be laid for subsequently much larger steps, all towards the destination of a low carbon future.

At the outset, it is important to emphasise the criticality of the role of the government. There is no other entity capable of creating the appropriate ecosystem for catalysing this initial movement. The government is required to create the enabling incentives. It will have to weigh in against the inertial tendencies of incumbent vested interests; to develop the regulatory systems and processes that encourage entrepreneurialism and, at the same time, check the excesses of the market; to encourage the search for new technology horizons; and perhaps, most importantly, find a way of balancing the demands of its domestic constituency with the imperatives of ecological balance. This may be an obvious point but it cannot be over-emphasised that' in the drive towards a low carbon future, the government will have to lead from the front.

This leads to the second proposition that, to weaken the linkage between energy demand and environmental degradation, the policy on energy must be developed holistically and not through the siloed processes of State politics, bureaucratic verticals and vested interests. This will require a major institutional overhaul and that might be a stretch too far in this initial phase. However, to lay the ground work and, in particular, to create awareness of the embedded interconnections between energy, environment and the macroeconomy, Indian parliament should legislate an omnibus "energy and environment responsibility act" and place the subject of energy and environment policy in the hands of a ministerial czar. The government has, in the past, legislated acts like the "fiscal responsibility act" and the "food security act" which placed a moral, if not a legal obligation, on governments, to exercise fiscal prudence and provide food to all. A similar legislation on energy would provide a platform for integrated discussions.

The third proposition is that local governments be empowered to act autonomously on issues related to energy efficiency, demand conservation, waste management, urban redesign and transportation. The current system of governance does provide municipal authorities such powers on paper. In practice, however, these powers have been straitjacketed by the tugs and pulls of electoral politics. The reality is that whilst municipal authorities have enormous powers to stymie progress — they can hold up files indefinitely — but have lost the powers to initiate new policy. Those powers are now vested with the politician whose priorities are dictated by the electoral cycle. This imbalance needs to be corrected.

Its first step is the vesting of energy management in an autonomous, constitutionally created, city energy ombudsman comparable to the Comptroller and Auditor General of India or the head of our Union Public Service Commission. The consultants McKenzie have done a report called "Deadline 2020". This report prioritises four action areas for cities — the decarbonisation of the electrical grid; the optimisation of energy efficiency; the development of next generation mobility; and the improvement of waste management. A similar study should be carried out for each of our tier-one cities and the identified actions should be the deliverables of this Ombudsman. The underlying objective of this proposition is to, on one hand, forewarn against one-size-fits-all macro solutions and, on the other hand, encourage the development and implementation of focused, small scale and distributed solutions.

The fourth proposition is to develop a raft of new financial products. The shift to a low carbon energy system requires investment in complementary infrastructure (smart cities, smart grids, smart meters, charging infrastructure, etc.), organisational restructuring and skill development. The investment levels are beyond the balance sheets of any Central or State government entity or indeed the private sector. And even if they were, the returns would be deemed too low and risky. However, there is no dearth of liquidity. The challenge is, therefore, to create the financing models to direct this money into "green investments". We have the financial and technology talent to develop such innovative financing techniques. What is required is to direct this talent towards the fulfilment of this objective.

The fifth proposition is akin to the fourth. India needs to place greater emphasis on clean energy R&D. It can, of course, hope to piggy back on the research that is being carried out across the world. However, that would lead to a relationship of dependency. Today, the competitiveness of our solar and electric vehicle initiatives depends on the availability of cheap Chinese-made solar photovoltaic panels and lithium ion batteries. The Chinese products are the cheapest available because China has invested substantially in battery technology and in the creation of photovoltaic manufacturing capacity. Were India to impose countervailing duties on Chinese imports, it would 'kill' the economics of India's domestic solar and electric vehicle investors. However, if these products are allowed unfettered entry, it would create a relationship of import dependency on a country with which India has a somewhat ambivalent relationship.

India has a "clean energy" fund to finance clean energy research. The fund is well endowed. The money in this fund has, however, not been used for clean energy research. Instead, it has been diverted to bridge budgetary deficits or some politically-favoured project like the cleansing of River

Ganges. This diversion should be stopped. India has capable technocrats. What it does not have is an enabling R&D ecosystem. Therefore, India should create such a system and initiate primary research on third generation, new horizon and clean energy technologies and in partnership with international universities, research laboratories, government entities and private scholars.

The final proposition is, in some ways, doff to the existing system. The inevitability of India's dependence on coal, oil and gas does not provide the luxury to trundle along in the hope that development now would allow India to clean up later. So, as India moves towards a non-fossil fuel-based energy system, the government is urged to look to "greening" India's current fossil fuel portfolio. There are many prongs to this effort, including the gasification of coal but one, in particular, needs to be placed on an immediate fast track, that is, the development of a national gas grid. Currently, much of South and East India have limited or no access to gas because of the inadequacy of the pipeline infrastructure. The Central government is aware of the importance of creating such a grid but its efforts have been constrained by the difficulties related to land acquisition and "rights of way" to lay the pipeline; the public perception that "gas" poses a risk to safety; finance and competitive politics between the Centre and the various States.

The former Prime Minister of the United Kingdom, Winston Churchill, once remarked that an era of procrastination will inevitably lead to an era of consequences. The Indian government needs to heed this forewarning and put the weight of its power behind efforts to remove these roadblocks.

Conclusion

India knows it has an energy and environment problem. It knows what needs to be done. It also knows that the transition to a different energy system will not be smooth but dissonant, disruptive and possibly dislocatory. However, it no longer has a choice! It has to forge a new social, institutional, regulatory and legislative contract for energy. It has to invent a new energy future and navigate towards this destination.

End Notes

1. "How Delhi became the most polluted city on Earth", Umair Irfan, *Vox*, 25 November 2017. https://www. vox.com/energy-and-environment/ 2017/11/22/16666808/india-air-pollution-new-delhi, accessed November 28, 2017.
2. Some of these consequences include stronger hurricanes and severe heat waves; crop damage due to higher heat levels; reduced water availability due to rising temperatures, changing precipitation patterns and increasing droughts; health issues due to heat waves, air pollution and diseases linked to climate; damage to forests, and animal and plant life due to shifting weather patterns, drought and wildfires. https://archive.epa. gov/climatechange/kids/ basics/today/greenhouse-gases.html, accessed December 23, 2017.
3. The Paris accord was negotiated by representatives of 196 parties at the 21st Conference of the Parties of the United Nations Framework Convention on Climate Change in Paris, France, and was adopted by consensus on 12 December 2015. As of November 2017, 195 members have signed the agreement, and 171 have become party to it. http://unfccc.int/paris_agreement/items/9444.php, accessed December 12, 2017.
4. Comin, Diego, and Hobijn, Bart. "An Exploration of Technology Diffusion", *American Economic Review* 100(5)(2010): 2031–2059. https://www.dartmouth. edu/~dcomin/files/exploration_ technology.pdf, accessed December 23, 2017.

Chapter 9

India's Belated Energy Transitions: Prospects for Leapfrogging to Low Carbon Sources

Lydia Powell

Introduction

Historically India's energy concerns have been dominated by external supply risks — particularly oil supply risks — because these were closely linked to two of India's key strategic interests — national security and rapid development through economic growth. India's response consisted of traditional policy interventions such as self-sufficiency, stockpiling and development of non-fossil alternatives such as nuclear power and renewable energy.

Though oil supply concerns continue to influence energy policy, India's current energy interventions centre around three energy transitions that are expected to alter India's traditional energy landscape. The slow but steady progress in energy access is enabling millions of poor households to shift to modern energy sources such as electricity and liquid petroleum gas (LPG). The "market" transition initiated in the 1990s is opening up a larger role for forces such as price, demand and supply to decide the direction and quantity of energy flows and energy investment. The low carbon

transition initiated about a decade ago is increasing the share of low carbon fuels, particularly renewable energy sources in India's energy basket.

While the rationales for each of the three transitions cannot be
contested, there are inherent contradictions. Past and present programmes for universal energy access are dependent on grid-based supply of electricity for lighting and petroleum-based fuels for heating
(primarily cooking). This means an increase in the use of fossil fuels.
On the other hand, the low carbon transition aims to shift India's
energy basket away from fossil fuels particularly away from coal by
increasing the share of renewable energy sources. This contradicts the
energy access transition based on fossil fuels. In the absence of a price
for environmental externalities such as carbon-di-oxide (CO_2) emissions, the market transition also favours fossil fuels, especially domestic
coal to meet growth demand for electricity and petroleum-based fuels
for transport and household use.

In both the low carbon transition and the energy access transition, the
government is the agent of change. Government interventions to facilitate
energy access and to increase the share of low carbon energy fuels are justified as the market is said to have failed to (i) provide equitable access to
energy and (ii) prevent negative environmental externalities of high carbon
energy production and use. The persistence of government interventions in
the energy sector contradicts the market transition that was initiated in the
late 1990s to address "state failure" (government failure) to increase production and supply of energy and to correct government failure in improving
technical and economic efficiency of energy use (Figure 1).

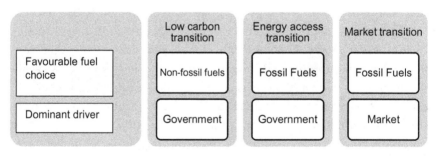

Figure 1:   Transitions in the energy sector.
Note: Assuming that there are no carbon taxes/penalties.

This paper evaluates the prospects for each of the transitions and makes an assessment of whether de-centralised low carbon technologies such as solar power would enable India to "leap-frog" into a market-driven, energy-abundant low carbon economy with little or no trade-offs.

The Energy Access Transition

The energy access transition in India is primarily a household level transition that is expected to eventually replace wood and other forms of bio-mass with petroleum-based fuels such as LPG as fuel for cooking and substitute oil lamps with electric bulbs for lighting. While most of India's peers completed the energy access transition decades ago, the transition is yet to be completed in India and this is casting a shadow on India's market transition and also on its low carbon transition.

At the time of independence, electricity generation and distribution were primarily in the hands of the private sector. Private companies and their franchisees focussed on urban and industrial demand which gave them a reasonable return on investment. Rural and agricultural sectors were ignored as they were seen as unprofitable. Only one in 200 villages were electrified and just 3% of the population in six large towns consumed over 56% of utility electricity.[1] Only 350 out of 856 towns with more than 10,000 people were electrified (Figure 2).[2]

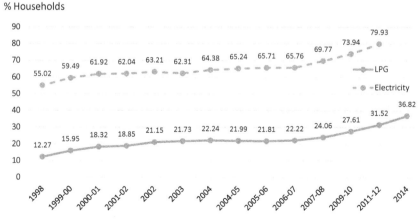

Figure 2:   Indian household access to modern energy sources 1998–2014.
Source: NSSO surveys various rounds.

The per person electricity consumption was 14 kWh per year and in many states the per person consumption was as low as 1 kWh per year.[3] In 2017, the average per person consumption of electricity was over 1000 kWh per year.[4] While the growth in average per person electricity consumption is impressive, the absolute value is still below world average energy consumption levels. The average per person energy consumption also hides wide disparities in electricity consumption between regions and consumer groups (urban and rural and industrialised and agricultural regions for example).

The total electricity consumption of the city of Delhi that has a population of about 18 million is more than that of the state of Bihar that has a population of more than 100 million.[5] Average per person electricity consumption on the basis of household surveys is still low at just over 240 kWh per person per year.[6] About a fifth of Indian households are expected to have the first electric light bulb installed only by 2018 or later.[7] The supply of electricity to two-thirds of Indian households in rural and semi-urban areas that are technically connected to the grid is intermittent and unreliable in terms of both quantity and quality.

Almost all of India's rural electrification programmes are driven by the government and are based on extending the electricity grid to un-electrified parts of the country. In the 1970s, the "minimum needs programme" aimed to provide minimum needs including electricity to rural households.[8] In the 1980s, an integrated rural energy plan aimed to provide a basket of solutions including grid-based electricity, petroleum products, fuel-wood and renewable energy sources to rural households.[9] The Kutir Jyoti[10] programme launched in the late 1980s offered a single point light (60 W) to all "below poverty level" (BPL) households with 100% grant.[11] Pradan Mantri Gramodaya Yojana (PMGY)[12] launched in the early 2000s offered states a role in implementing the electrification programme with most of the funding from the federal government. The "Rajiv Gandhi Grameen Vidyudikaran Yojana" (RGGVY), a scheme launched in 2005 by the federal government which subsumed all earlier schemes for electrification aimed to provide "electricity to all" in 5 years. The "Deendayal Upadhyaya Gram Jyoti Yojana (DDUGJY)" scheme launched in 2014 by the current government merely repackages the RGGVY under a new name.

Even as recently as 2017, the government continued to roll out schemes such as the "Sahaj Bijli Har Ghar Yojana"[13] or the "Saubhagya" scheme to provide electricity connections to over 40 million families in rural and urban areas by December 2018 based on grid extensions. This means that roughly 15% of the households (or about 220 million people) were not physically connected to the grid despite seven decades of government interventions. In roughly 100 million households located in rural areas that have a physical link to the grid, electricity supply continues to be irregular and unpredictable.[14]

Policy treated electricity as a public good but the issue of how the cost of supplying this good will be recovered was not discussed or clarified. State Electricity Boards (SEBs) that held the mandate of increasing electricity access to households were "administrations" rather than commercial enterprises and thus were not subjected to economic evaluation.[15] Under the Electricity Supply Act of 1948, SEBs were only expected to earn a return of 3% on their net fixed assets in services after meeting other financial obligations and depreciation. This provision enabled SEBs to accelerate rural electrification in India but the key driver behind rural electrification programmes in the mid-1960s and 1970s was the strategic goal of increasing domestic food production. Rural electricity supply was intended for pumps that sucked up ground water for irrigating agricultural land rather than for lighting up impoverished rural households.[16] However, the extension of the grid to irrigate land did facilitate household electrification to some extent. Though electricity-based ground water pumping and village electrification accelerated in this period, SEBs began to falter financially in the late 1960s. In 1964 an expert committee recommended that SEBs should aim for a return of 11% but this recommendation was not implemented.[17] Schemes of subsidies and hand-outs from the respective state governments were devised to enable SEBs to continue functioning.[18] These schemes failed to revive the financial fortunes of SEBs and consequently losses and debt continued to build up. Accumulated financial liabilities of SEBs estimated at about Rs. 4.3 trillion in 2014–2015[19] are now seen as one of the key inhibiting factors in the ongoing energy transitions.

In the context of the energy access transition, SEBs that are now expected to operate as commercial entities under India's market transition have no economic incentive to supply electricity to rural households. This is partly because regulated tariff for electricity does not cover the cost of supply and partly because rural household electricity loads are not sufficiently large to justify continuous high quality electricity supply.

In the context of the low carbon transition, SEBs alone are unable to bear the system level cost of accommodating intermittent renewable energy sources. SEBs have not necessarily welcomed the "must run" status accorded to renewable energy as it compromises on the power purchase agreements (PPAs) signed with conventional power generators and imposes additional costs.[20] SEBs have also attempted to resist feed-in tariff for renewable energy as additional costs cannot be easily passed on to consumers under the existing regulatory framework.[21] The draft national energy policy (NEP) released in 2017 observes that SEBs cannot be burdened with the social and system cost of accommodating renewable energy sources and recommends finding alternative mechanisms for meeting additional costs.[22]

Provisions for prioritising renewable energy also go against federal incentive schemes for financial restructuring of SEBs such as the government's Ujwal Discom Assurance Yojana (UDAY) scheme. Ironically, one of the incentives that the UDAY scheme offers to SEBs for adopting market discipline in their operations is greater access to low cost domestic coal. The rationale is that this would enable SEBs to increase electricity access.

The transition from biomass to modern cooking fuels such as LPG not only had a much later start but followed a much slower pace than that of the transition from oil lamps to electric bulbs. In the 1950s, almost all households used firewood and dried animal dung as fuel for cooking. In the 1970s, LPG stoves started replacing kerosene stoves in urban households when new refineries in India started producing bottled LPG. In 1977, there were only 3.2 million LPG connections across India (or 2.5% of the households) had access to LPG.[23] In 1984, the number of LPG connections had tripled to 8.8 million (5% of the households) and in 1990 the number of LPG connections increased to 19.6 million (11% of the households). The growth in LPG connections at over 14% in the period between 1977 and 1990 was above that for electricity although it was from a very small base.[24] A number of state governments launched dedicated programmes for distribution of subsidised or free LPG connections to the so called "below poverty line" (BPL) households. The Rajiv Gandhi Gramin LPG Vitran (RGGLV) scheme launched in 2009 more than doubled LPG dealers in rural areas.[25]

According to household level surveys made in 2015–2016, 40% of households in India have access to LPG today but most of these households are in urban areas.[26] About 18% of rural households use LPG as their primary fuel for cooking along with other fuels, dried animal dung and kerosene. Data on household connections registered by retail LPG dealers suggests that about 80% of the households have access to LPG but this figure assumes that LPG connections are distributed equally among households which is not necessarily accurate.[27]

Despite the inconsistency in the data, the broader trend of dramatic growth in the adoption of LPG in semi-urban and rural households in the last few years cannot be disputed. Domestic LPG consumption has grown at over 9% per year since 2011 and it is expected to grow by over 15% in 2016–2017. India's LPG imports are expected to increase by 2 million tonnes (mt) or nearly 17% year-on-year, to about 14 mt in fiscal 2018–2019 making India the second largest importer of LPG in the world.[28] Like electricity access programmes, LPG access programmes are also government driven and are funded by subsidies and grants. This places a large burden on public finances often channelled through public sector oil companies, especially in periods when global crude oil prices are high.

The shift from biomass to LPG by poor households is presented by the policy makers as a shift to cleaner fuels but this is a contested claim. Particulate matter emitted during the incomplete combustion of biomass in rudimentary cook stoves is seen as polluting the household and the local environment and LPG is seen as a cleaner burning alternative. While this is true at the household and local level, LPG is a fossil fuel which means it is associated with the emission of CO_2 during its production and use.[29] Biomass is generally considered a renewable fuel and also a carbon neutral fuel as the CO_2 emitted by plant matter in the process of burning is only the amount of CO_2 absorbed in the growing.[30]

The energy access transitions (electricity and LPG) are thus state driven transitions that expect to move households from traditional fuels to modern fossil fuel derived energy forms. In fact, the most significant change in India's energy basket in the next two decades is expected to be driven by the energy access transition under which the share of traditional fuels is expected to fall from 22% today to about 15% in 2040.[31] As per current trends most of the shift away from traditional fuels is towards fossil fuels.

The Market Transition

Historically India has considered the energy sector to be too important to be left to the market. Soon after independence India consolidated its hold over the oil and gas industry which, until then, was dominated by a few Anglo-American companies.[32] The industrial policy resolution of 1948 and 1956 clearly stated the government's aspiration and future plans for core industries like petroleum with all future development reserved for public sector undertakings.[33] Electricity generation, transmission and distribution were also brought under government control immediately after independence as noted in the previous section.

The presumed absolute scarcity of primary energy resources justified state presence in the sector. In the case of hydrocarbons, the inadequacy of domestic resources that made India dependent on supposedly unreliable imported oil supplies was interpreted as a strategic vulnerability. This justified the heavy presence of the state in every segment of the hydrocarbon value chain.

State control of the energy sector created monopolies which underperformed technically, administratively and economically even though they had unquestionable rights over energy resources and were insulated from price uncertainty. This resulted in persistent energy shortfalls at one end and unsustainable financial liabilities at the other. Pressure for change built up but the trigger that opened up a larger role for markets in the energy (and other) sectors was the external payments crisis of 1991. The crisis made it clear that the attempt to insulate the country from market forces through price controls as well as the strategy to hedge against geopolitical risks through government ownership and control of energy resources had failed to produce the desired outcomes such as energy security, affordability of energy and increased access to energy. To a large extent, the payments crisis was also an inevitable consequence of the fragile financial situation to which publicly controlled enterprises in the energy and heavy industry segments had contributed.[34]

Among the many fiscal policy reforms initiated in this period was the restructuring of public sector companies in the energy sector, curbing growth of contingent liabilities such as the oil pool account in 2002 and the dismantling of the administered price mechanism (APM) in the petroleum sector.[35] Several state governments initiated measures to reform the power sector to mobilise private sector resources for augmenting power generation capacity. Most of the states either constituted or notified the constitution of state electricity regulatory commissions (SERCs). Many states also proposed unbundling or corporatisation of their SEBs and many states signed MOUs with the federal government to undertake reforms in a time-bound manner.[36] The federal government made provisions for financial assistance to states under the Accelerated Power Development and Reform Programme (APDRP) scheme.[37] The Electricity Act enacted in 2003 de-licenced power generation, made competitive bidding mandatory for power procurement and introduced markets for trading electricity. A legal step was taken to ensure fiscal discipline and fiscal consolidation through the enactment of the Fiscal Responsibility and Budget Management Act (FRBM) in 2003. Effectively the FRBM Act put limits on the ability of governments at the state and central levels to finance revenue deficits for through borrowing.[38] For the energy sector, this meant that policies for energy access based entirely on subsidies or grants had to be curtailed. On the hydrocarbon side, the enactment of the Petroleum & Natural Gas Regulatory Act of 2006 facilitated the establishment of the Petroleum & Natural Gas Regulatory Board (PNGRB) that had a mandate to regulate downstream activities of the oil and natural gas sector.[39]

Economic boundaries set by the FRBM Act were often breached on account of unprecedented economic headwinds such as a substantial increase in oil prices and the global financial crisis of 2008, but the overall direction of market-oriented reform continues to have an impact on the investment, production, supply and pricing of energy and energy services. Likewise, the market-enabling provisions of the Electricity Act 2003 and Petroleum & Natural Gas Regulatory Act of 2006 are yet to unravel fully but their influence in shaping a market-oriented energy sector cannot be denied.

The market transition and the consequent influence of commercial considerations may have a negative impact on India "leap-frogging" to a low carbon economy. Solar and wind energy prices have reached parity with traditional coal-based power at the "bus-bar" level (plant level) but these energy sources are yet to reach parity at the "grid" or "retail" level. Until then renewable resources would remain dependent on subsidies. How market forces would influence the flow of subsidies and investment to renewable energy sources is unclear at this point. The market transition will sustain the low carbon or the energy access transition only when solar and wind energy with storage back up emerge as commercial competition to grid-based electricity in providing 24 h uninterrupted electricity supply.[40]

Low Carbon Transition

The pursuit of low carbon growth, narrowly defined as increasing the share of non-fossil fuel energy sources was initiated in response to international demand for limiting CO_2 emissions. Fossil fuels (coal, oil and gas) currently constitute 75% of India's primary energy basket (which includes traditional energy sources) in 2016.[41] 22% of the energy basket is from traditional fuels such as fire-wood and biomass. The remaining 3% is from non-fossil fuel energy sources such as nuclear energy, hydropower and renewable energy.

The budget for 2015–2016 announced by the new government revised the target for renewable energy capacity to 175 GW by 2022 that included 100 GW of solar (from about 17 GW today), 60 GW of wind (from about 32 GW today), 10 GW of biomass 5 GW of small hydro-power.[42] The government also increased the target for solar water pumps to over 100,000 from less than a 1,000 today. To reach the overall target set for renewable or low carbon energy, India would have to develop, in just 7 years renewable energy capacity that exceeds coal-based generation capacity that India developed in the last 60 years (Figure 3).

According to projections by the International Energy Agency (IEA), the share of fossil fuels in India's primary energy basket is expected to increase to 82% by 2040 from 75% in 2016 under a business as usual (BAU) scenario.[43] The share of fossil fuels is expected to increase marginally to 77% under the new policies scenario where policies such as India's

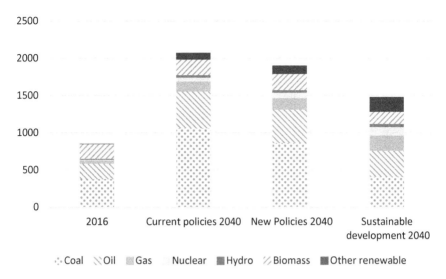

Figure 3: Projections for primary energy sources IEA.
Source: World Energy Outlook 2017, IEA.

commitment to the Paris Agreement and India's commitment (non-binding) to install 175 GW of renewable energy generation capacity by 2022 have an impact. Under a 'sustainable development' scenario, the share of fossil fuels is estimated to fall to 66% by 2040.

According to projections by the draft national energy policy (NEP) by Niti Aayog[44] renewable and clean energy sources are expected to account for just over 8% of primary energy supply in 2040 under the BAU scenario and 13% under an ambitious scenario.[45] In other words, the share of fossil fuels is expected to increase from 81% in 2012 to 92% by 2040 in the BAU scenario and increase to 87% in the "ambitious" scenario (Figure 4).

The share of fossil fuels increases in both the BAU and ambitious scenario of the draft NEP whereas the share of fossil fuels decreases in the sustainable development scenario of the IEA. The share of low carbon or non-fossil fuel energy sources does not increase significantly under both Niti Aayog scenarios. As the two scenarios reflect the upper and lower bound for fossil fuels, the important unanswered questions in the draft NEP is why the share of fossil fuels is high even when the assumptions fed into the quantitative model capture all low carbon policies of the government.

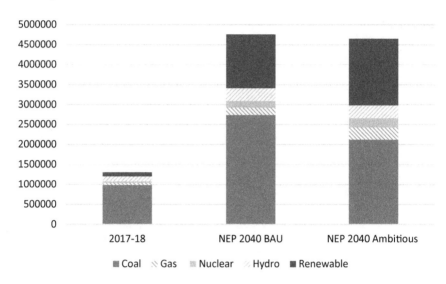

Figure 4:   Projections for fuels for power generation NEP.
Source: Draft National Energy Policy of the Niti Aayog.

Coal currently accounts for 45% of India's primary energy basket and 76% of electricity generation. Fossil fuels (coal, oil and gas) account for 83% of power generated in 2016 but this share is expected to fall to 26% by 2040 under the sustainable growth scenario of IEA (which is pitched as the most desirable but difficult path) with power generation by solar photovoltaic (PV) cells alone exceeding the share of power generation by fossil fuels. The share of fossil fuels (coal and gas) in power generation is expected to fall to 55% under the scenario where new policies are implemented (Figure 5).

Under a BAU scenario the share of fossil fuels is expected to fall to 52%. Ironically the BAU scenario of the IEA leads to a lower share of fossil fuels than the new policies scenario which factors in low carbon targets set by the new government. A possible reason is that the BAU scenario does not factor in polices to provide universal access to electricity and modern cooking fuels which are mostly based on fossil fuels. The draft NEP projects the share of fossil fuels in electricity generation to fall to about 61% by 2040 under the BAU scenario and fall to just over 50% under the "ambitious" scenario.

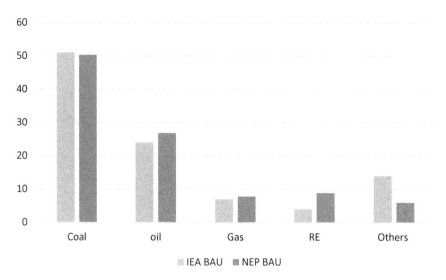

Figure 5:   Projections for primary energy shares by 2040 NEP & IEA.
Source: Draft National Energy Policy Report and World Energy Outlook 2017 (IEA).

The projections for 2040 summarised do not capture all welfare and other macroeconomic or socio-economic costs that would have to be factored in for scenarios other than that of BAU. Broader macroeconomic costs such as balancing costs for managing intermittency of renewable energy, the cost of stranded assets (e.g., the capital and finance costs associated with existing power stations in the context of transitioning to renewable energy sources or the capital and finance cost of refineries and refinery upgradation in the case of transitioning to electric vehicles [EVs]), and the policy costs associated with regulating and enforcing future policy, the impact of lower comfort levels in buildings, inconvenience of travelling less or that of using public transport, research and development (R&D) costs are not taken into account. Implications such as revenue loss on account of fuel shifts and social consequences of massive job losses in the coal sector are also not taken into account. In the next two decades, India's low carbon transition is thus likely to decrease the share of fossil fuels compared to the business as usual scenario rather than replace fossil fuels completely. The carbon content in India's energy system is likely to be *lower* in the next two decades but whether this constitutes a *low* carbon transition could be a matter of perception.

Conclusions

India's three simultaneous transitions appear to be working at cross purposes in the broader context. The former two transitions seek to increase the quantity of energy supplies and the latter seeks to improve the quality of energy supplies. If both quantity and quality improvements are achieved, it may come at the cost of providing equitable access to energy. It may also involve a trade-off on the market transition. How India balances these trade-offs will decide the nature and direction of India's energy trajectory in the future.

The juxtaposition of a technological transition with political, social and economic transitions makes it difficult to determine where policy will end and politics will begin. The economic transformation requires the state to exit the energy sector so that the market can mediate supply of and demand for energy. The social transformation requires the state to continue its presence in the energy sector to correct market failure in providing universal access to energy. The environmental transformation also requires the state to correct market failure in providing a clean environment.

In general, optimism over all three transitions making substantial progress in the next two decades is justified. In the context of domestic politics the energy access and market transitions which are essentially quantitative transitions are likely to succeed to a greater extent than the low carbon transition. From an international political and technocratic perspective the low carbon transition may succeed in the limited sense that it replaces a share of fossil fuels.

The global endeavour to limit carbon emissions is reshaping the narrative on India's "energy problem" that are essentially internal political and economic problems as a technological problem. Under this narrative, technology that includes low carbon and information technologies becomes the tool for mediating social, political and economic problems including the energy justice problem.

An intriguing prospect is that the entrenched role of the state in the Indian energy sector that has until now been seen as one of the key weaknesses of the sector, may prove to be a strength in accelerating the transition towards a low carbon economy. The key uncertainty here is whether this transition would involve a compromise on other broader policy goals of the government such as rapid economic growth through industrialisation and the provision of universal access to energy.

Looking back into history there is a case for optimism over India "leap-frogging" into low carbon energy sources. Global energy transitions in the past were not driven by cost competitiveness. Diffusion of technologies at the demand end with consumers wanting convenience and cleanliness drove the shift to refined petroleum and grid-based energy forms (natural gas and electricity).[46] India's low carbon transition could also be driven by consumer preference for de-centralised clean energy rather than by substitution at the supply end as it is envisaged today.

End Notes

1. Planning Commission, "First Five Year Plan (1951–1956)", Government of India (1951).
2. *Ibid.*
3. *Ibid.*
4. Central Electricity Authority (CEA), "Growth of Electricity Sector from 1947 to 2017", Government of India, Ministry of Power (2017).
5. Calculated using data from the Central Electricity Authority.
6. Calculated using data for household electricity consumption (CEA), number of households (Census of India), average household size (census of India).
7. *Economic Times*, "Electricity for All by 2018, All Villages to be electrified this year: Power Minister", September 25, 2017, https://economictimes. indiatimes.com/industry/energy/power/power-for-all-by-december-2018-all-villages-to-be-electrified-this-year-power-minister/articleshow/60830923. cms
8. Planning Commission, "Fifth Five Year Plan (1974–1978)", Government of India (1974).
9. Planning Commission, "Sixth Five Year Plan (1980–1985)", Government of India (1980).
10. *'Lighting up huts'*.
11. Press Information Bureau (PIB), 'Electricity Connection to Tribal People', August 12, 2005. http://pib.nic.in/newsite/erelcontent.aspx?relid=11231.

12. *'Prime Ministers Plan for Villages'.*
13. *'Affordable Electricity to all Households'.*
14. http://watchyourpower.org/.
15. Ruet, Joel, *Privatizing Power Cuts: Ownership and Reform of State Electricity Boards in India* (India: Academic Foundation, 2005).
16. Powell, Lydia, "India's Energy Security: The Government's Role", *Dialogue* 149(3) (2013).
17. Kale, S Sunila, *Electrifying India: Regional Political Economies of Development* (California: Stanford University Press, 2014).
18. Third and fourth plan documents.
19. Ghose, Payal and Raja, Aparna N, "Ujwal Discom Assurance Yojana", *CCIL Monthly News Letter* (August 2016).
20. Jai, Shreya Jai, "In a first, Madhya Pradesh takes away must-run status of renewable projects", *Business Standard* New Delhi, August 4, 2017, http://www.business-standard.com/article/economy-policy/in-a-first-madhya-pradesh-takes-away-must-run-status-of-renewable-projects-117080200409_1.html.
21. Rajat Ubhaykar, "Sunshine Or Sunstroke?, Outlook, Business, August 4, 2016. https://www.outlookbusiness.com/the-big-story/lead-story/sunshine-or-sunstroke-2931.
22. Niti Aayog, 'Draft National Energy Policy' (Government of India, 2017).
23. Planning Commission, *Seventh Five Year Plan (1986-90)*, Volume II (Energy, Government of India, 1985).
24. Data from 6th, 7th and 8th plan documents.
25. https://indane.co.in/rgglvs.php.
26. Data compiled from National Sample Survey Database.
27. Petroleum Planning and Analysis Cell, 'LPG Profile', Ministry of Petroleum, Government of India, 2018.
28. Platts, 'India's LPG imports expected to hit 14 million tonnes in fiscal 2018-19', February 20, 2018. https://www.platts.com/latest-news/petrochemicals/singapore/feature-indias-lpg-imports-expected-to-hit-14-26894705.
29. There is temporal inconsistency between CO_2 absorption and emission. The time taken for CO_2 absorption is longer than the time taken for carbon emission by orders of magnitude and many in the scientific community believe that biomass burning will have an impact on CO_2 accumulation in the atmosphere.
30. Harvey, Chelsea and Nina Heikkinen, 'Congress Says Biomass is Carbon-Neutral, but Scientists Disagree: Using wood as fuel source could actually increase CO_2 emissions', Scientific American, E&E News, March 23, 2018.

31. International Energy Agency, World Energy Outlook 2017 (Paris, 2017).
32. Visvanath, Dr S N, *A Hundred Years of Oil* (Oil India Limited, New Delhi: Vikas Publishing House, 1997).
33. Bhatia, R, *Planning for Petroleum & Fertilizer Industries: Programming Model for India* (New Delhi: Oxford University Press, 1983).
34. Reserve Bank of India (RBI), 'Report on Fiscal Policy' (2003), https://www.rbi.org.in/scripts/PublicationReportDetails.aspx?ID=326.
35. *Ibid.*
36. Shahi, R V., "Infrastructure Reforms in India: A Case Study of the Power Sector", in Narayan S (Ed.), *Documenting Reforms: Case Studies from India* (Macmillan in association with the Observer Research Foundation, 2006).
37. Press Information Bureau, 'Reforms in the Power Sector', Ministry of Power, Government of India, December 1, 2014,
38. Singh, Charan and Devi Prasad, K K Sharma, Shivkumara Reddy, 'A Review of the FRBM Act', IIM Bangalore Working Paper Number 550, June 2017.
39. Narayan, S., 'Reforms in the Oil & Gas Sector' in Narayan S (Ed.), *Documenting Reforms: Case Studies from India* (Macmillan in association with the Observer Research Foundation, 2006).
40. Frank, Charles, 'The Net benefit of Low and No Carbon Electricity Technologies, Global Economy & Development Working Paper No 73, Brookings Institution, March 2014.
41. Niti Aayog. Draft National Energy Policy. Version as on 27.06.2017 (New Delhi: Government of India, 2017).
42. Ministry of Finance, 'Key Features of the Budget 2015–16' (Government of India, 2015).
43. International Energy Agency, 'World Energy Outlook 2017 (Paris, 2017).
44. Formerly the Planning Commission of the Government of India.
45. Niti Aayog, "Draft National Energy Policy", Version as on 27.06.2017 (New Delhi: Government of India, 2017).
46. Unger, Richard, W, "Energy Transitions in History: Global Cases of Continuity and Change", *Racheal Carson Centre Perspectives* (2013).

Chapter 10

Solar Energy Financing in India

Amitendu Palit*

Introduction

Sustainable Development Goals (SDGs) entail the significant challenge of transitioning to clean sources of energy consumption. But the goal of making clean energy, i.e., non-fossil fuel and renewable energy, the main sources of energy consumption for countries, societies and economies cannot be achieved without addressing the challenge of mobilising finance for these energy projects.

Financing for clean energy is now a high global priority. The issue of financing renewable energy, particularly solar energy, has achieved great salience after the coming into force of the Paris Agreement on climate change from November 4, 2016. The Paris Agreement commits to: "Making finance flows consistent with a pathway towards low greenhouse gas emissions and climate-resilient development".[1]

*An earlier version of the paper was published by the Research and Information System for Developing Countries (RIS), Delhi India as a Discussion Paper: Amitendu Palit, *Financing Solar Energy: Lessons from Indian Experience*, RIS-DP #226, Research and Information System for Developing Countries, April 2018. The author is grateful to Ms Roshni Kapur, Research Analyst at the Institute of South Asian Studies (ISAS), National University of Singapore (NUS) for her excellent research assistance.

As of July 13, 2018, 179 countries accounting for around 89% of global emissions have ratified the Paris Agreement.[2] The widespread response has made the objective of mobilising climate finance consistent with the goals of sustainable economic development become core parts of national economic development agendas of the ratifying countries. Among these countries, the imperative for organising adequate finance for renewables is high for emerging markets, as they are on the cusp of climate adaptation and aiming to achieve the correct mix of technology and environment policies for addressing mitigation and adaptation.

From an emerging market and developing country perspective, the financing challenge is substantial. This is evident from the fact that initial investments in renewable energy projects take considerable time to mature and generate returns. This is characteristic of almost all "new generation" infrastructure projects that involve long gestation lags before yielding returns. As a result, bank finance for renewable energy projects are priced at higher rates than those to fossil-fuel-based projects like coal-fired thermal electricity plants. Financial terms are also more expensive due to higher capital costs for these projects.

High interest rates are a hindrance to expansion of renewable energy projects in many developing economies, where cost of credit and finance can substantially impact the production cost of renewable energy leading to high prices of such energy for consumers. Longer cost–benefit scenario horizons and asset–liability mismatches make it difficult for private investors to consider renewable energy projects. On the other hand, government support through subsidies to develop renewables, while essential, cannot be assumed perpetual.

The challenge for policymakers is to ensure that adequate alternative mechanisms and options exist for financing renewables. These, though, need to be attractive for private investors since the state subsidies for building renewables cannot be expected to last beyond the first few years of the projects. At the same time, an active role of the state in drawing up a constructive policy framework for encouraging clean energy investments is imperative.

Green bonds have emerged as an attractive option for financing renewables. India has made important strides in this regard, particularly in mobilising funds for solar energy projects. While India is still experimenting with regulations, modes of finance and pricing mechanisms, its rapid addition to renewable energy capacity — through solar power — underscores the success it has begun acquiring, and the rising pre-eminence of green bonds. India's efforts and experience provide important pointers to the global goal of pushing ahead on clean energy, through landmark initiatives like the International Solar Alliance of more than 100 solar power resource rich countries located between the Tropic of Cancer and Tropic of Capricorn,[3] which India is spearheading with France.

Solar Energy in India

India's quest for increasing installed capacity of solar energy began from the Jawaharlal Nehru National Solar Mission (JNNSM) launched in 2010. During the initial launch, the target was 20 GW by 2022. The objective brought to light the importance of mobilising finance for solar energy developers as well as the support that the government needed to provide to the initiative.

In recent years, India has made notable progress in restructuring the pattern of its domestic energy consumption towards energy from renewable sources. It has an ambitious target of expanding its current renewable energy capacity of 58–175 GW by 2022. The main contributions to the expansion are from new capacities of 100 GW solar energy and 60 GW of wind energy. These ambitious targets by India have made a significant influence on the global outlook for new capacities in renewable energy. According to the International Atomic Energy (IEA), global renewable energy capacity is expected to increase by 1,000 MW by 2022. Much of this increase is expected from China and India with the latter more than doubling its capacity of renewable energy over the next 5 years.[4]

As on March 31, 2017, the total potential for renewable power generation in India was 1,001,142 MW. The solar power potential was nearly 65% of this pool estimated at 649,342 MW.[5] Keeping in line with the potential, solar power has experienced the most rapid growth among renewables, in India. On a year-on-year basis, India's installed capacity in solar power almost doubled from 6.76 GW from 2015–2016 to 12.28 GW in 2016–2017[6] (Table 1). Solar power had the second highest installed generated capacity among renewable sources of power in India in

Table 1:   Installed capacity of grid interactive solar power (MW).

As on	Solar power
31.03.2008	2.12
31.03.2009	2.12
31.03.2010	10.28
31.03.2011	35.15
31.03.2012	941.24
31.03.2013	1686.44
31.03.2014	2631.96
31.03.2015	3743.99
31.03.2016	6762.85
31.03.2017	12288.83

Source: "Estimated Reserve And Installed Capacity Of Various Sources Of Energies", ENERGY — Statistical Year Book India 2018, Government of India-Statistics and Programme Implementation, http://mospi.nic.in/statistical-year-book-india/2018/185, accessed October 20, 2018.

2017 and accounted for more than 20% of the installed generation capacity, after wind power, which accounts for 56% of the capacity. The rapid increase in installed capacity of solar power has not only increased its use, but has also helped in decreasing its cost.[7] It is important for India to maintain the double virtues of higher production accompanied by lower cost. Financing options are key in this regard.

Two structural segments have driven the rapid growth in solar power. The first of these are relatively larger utility-scale projects of more than 1 MW in capacity. The second are smaller roof-top projects with capacities between 1 KW and 1 MW. Both these categories are experiencing rapid expansion from burgeoning commercial and industrial demand. Household demand for renewable energy is also increasing. As can be seen from Table 1, the installed capacity of grid interactive renewable power has had a particularly rapid growth since 2012. At the same time, solar power produced by off-grid smaller units have also increased rapidly, not just through power plants, but also in solar lanterns and street lighting systems (Table 2).

Table 2:   Installation of off-grid/de-centralised renewable energy system/devices.

| As on | Solar Photovoltaic (SPV) system | | | |
	SLS (Nos. In lakh)	HLS (Nos. In lakh)	SL (Nos. In lakh)	PP (KWP)
31.03.2009	0.6	3.6	5.6	2180
31.03.2010	8.0	6.0	1.2	2922
31.03.2011	2.0	7.5	7.3	9143
31.03.2012	2.3	8.9	9.3	23431
31.03.2013	2.6	9.9	9.4	48169
31.03.2014	2.7	11.0	9.6	85138
31.03.2015	3.4	12.0	9.9	109753
31.03.2016	4.0	12.9	10.0	140862
31.03.2017	4.7	14.0	10.0	176847

Note: SLS = Street Lighting Systems; HLS = Home Lighting System; Sl = Solar Lantern; PP = Power Plants; SPV = Solar Photovoltaic.
Source: "Estimated Reserve And Installed Capacity Of Various Sources Of Energies", ENERGY — Statistical Year Book India 2018, Government of India-Statistics and Programme Implementation, http://mospi.nic.in/statistical-year-book-india/2018/185, accessed October 20, 2018.

Financing Solar Power Growth

During the current decade, India's quest for mobilising finance for renewable energy has passed through several phases. Beginning from an initial situation of extending active state support to development of the solar power industry, India has graduated to having a domestic solar industry whose prospects for mobilising finance have improved considerably. At the same time, from being an industry burdened by high consumer tariffs inflicted by development costs, India's solar industry has transitioned to one with astonishingly low tariffs. In the process, the industry has experienced new regulatory and development challenges with respect to its financial prospects.

State support

The Indian experience draws attention to the importance of the state providing active support in accelerating the first-generation of investments for developing solar power. In India, this began from initial introduction of state subsidies for supporting solar power development. The subsidies, provided under a viability gap arrangement, aimed to cover a third of the project costs with further attention on covering capital costs that could not be recovered from tariffs.[8] The viability gap funding mechanism has been followed up by more elaborate subsidy provision through the Payment Security Fund (PSF). The PSF — administered by the Solar Energy Corporation of India Ltd — is worth US$220 million and aims to protect and safeguard developer interests. The scheme attempts to ensure developers do not suffer from delays or defaults with respect to their arrangements with grid and distribution companies and also extended to bank guarantees.

The importance of the PSF in an Indian context can hardly be over-emphasised. The PSF symbolises the Government of India's efforts to underwrite and protect solar power investments in the country. Much of this emphasis arises from the fact that infrastructure projects in India have suffered from delays as developers have been unable to honour commitments to financiers. The PSF aims to make sure such impediments do not inhibit solar power development, particularly if distribution companies are unable to pay on time for the power they buy from solar developers. However, at a time when both public and private banks in India are saddled with large non-performing loans arising from struggling infrastructure projects, the PSF's effectiveness needs to be carefully reviewed.

Reducing cost of finance

Renewable energy prices, particularly those of solar energy, are usually higher than fossil-fuel energy prices due to asset–liability mismatch and — as explained in the beginning — higher interest rate for clean energy finance. This often becomes a disincentive for developers as they are unsure about returns on their investment. Electricity distribution companies are also reluctant to buy expensive power as they wish to avoid passing on the higher charges to consumers.

For India, it has been imperative to identify alternative sources of mobilising finance to reduce reliance of developers on bank lending. The latter, for new energy projects in India, has become expensive due to exposures of Indian banks to coal-fired thermal plants, many of which have failed to take-off due to a variety of bottlenecks such as land acquisition leading to a build-up of non-performing loans.

Renewable energy developers in India, particularly in solar power, have been steadily shifting from bank loans to raising resources through bonds, mostly from international markets.[9] The cost of mobilising finance through 'green bonds' is much cheaper compared with bank loans. Even at fixed rates of 5% or a little more, the cost of debt financing from international markets remains lower than the cost of similar debt in the Indian domestic market as well as interest rates being charged by Indian banks. Even including exchange rate risks, the costs of international bonds would be lower than domestic bonds. The ability to raise finances from overseas investors through green bonds points to the possibility of India being able to meet its stated target of generating 175 GW of power from renewable sources by 2022.

Mainstreaming green bonds

Globally, the drive for clean energy finance has picked up considerable momentum through "green bonds". India has been one of the leading countries in this respect. India's experience has several important pointers in this regard. Green bonds are fixed-income debt instruments for mobilising financial resources to be utilised mostly for climate change mitigation and adaptation projects. It is the exclusive character of the utilisation of their proceeds that make these bonds different from other general bonds issued by various entities as debt instruments.

From the developer's perspective, green bonds are long-term low cost financing alternatives with exclusive focus on end-use. These are rational alternatives for attracting foreign investors to the domain of clean energy finance, particularly those looking for assured fixed returns in the medium and long-term horizons. Apart from assured returns, investors in green bonds are encouraged by prospects of higher future return on investments in such bonds given the greater use and competitiveness of renewable energy *vis-à-vis* fossil fuel energy.[10]

Green bond issuance has caught up fast in emerging markets. The Moody's investor service expect global green bonds issuance to surge to

US$250 billion in 2018 reflecting a growth of 60% over US$155 billion in 2017. Along with developed markets, emerging market economies, led by China and India are expected to contribute majorly to the global growth in green bonds issuance.

The green bond statistics for China and India are worth noting. The combined bond issuance by both countries, till now, are US$53 billion in the total global green bonds market.[11] In both countries, green bond issues have accelerated since the announcement of specific regulatory guidelines, such as by the Securities and Exchange Board of India (SEBI) in May 2017.

India introduced green bonds from February 2015 with YES Bank being the first financial institution to issue a green bond (Table 3). This was followed by an introduction of green bonds for funding clean and renewable energy projects by IFC and IDBI's issue of such bonds on the Singapore Stock Exchange later during that year. Axis Bank's green bond issue on London Stock Exchange happened soon after in June 2016. The first SEBI-approved green bond was issued by Larsen & Toubro in July 2017.[12]

The green bond market has grown bigger over time encompassing state-owned commercial banks, state-owned financial institutions and corporates.[13] Globally, among G20 countries, green bond issuance by India is on the increase with the country having one of the larger shares of green bonds in total corporate debt: India's share is 0.35%, which is higher than that of the European Union (0.29%), China (0.26%), Australia (0.19%), Canada (0.12%) and the United States (0.09%).[14]

Table 3 indicates the dominance of renewable energy for green bonds. Low carbon transport and water management are the other areas that have attracted green bonds. But energy exceeds the end-use purpose of green bonds, both for private and public issuers of such bonds in India. This becomes evident from a closer look at the bonds issued just for the year 2017 (Table 4). Out of a total of US$3.8 billion green bonds issued during that year, there was only one bond issue that included water among its end-use proceeds in addition to energy, while all others focused on energy (except one on transport).

The interest of both issuers as well as investors in green bonds is evident from the enthusiastic response to these bonds reflected in oversubscription of the bond issues (Table 5). The issue by IREDA in 2016 was

Table 3:   Indian green bonds 2015–March 2017.

Date	Issuer	Amount	Coupon	Tenor	Certified/ Reviewed	Theme
Feb 2015	Yes Bank	INR10 billion	8.85	10	n/a	Renewable energy and energy efficiency
Apr 2015	Export-Import Bank of India	US$500 m*	2.75	5	n/a	Low carbon transport
Sept 2015	CLP Wind Farms India	INR6.0 billion	9.15	3, 4 & 5	n/a	Renewable energy
Nov 2015	IDBI	US$350 m*	4.25	5	KPMG	Renewable energy, low carbon transport and water management
Feb 2016	Hero Future Energies	INR3.0 billion	10.75	3 & 6	Climate Bonds Standard	Renewable energy
April 2016	PNB Housing Finance	INR5.0 billion	8.01	n/a	n/a	Low carbon buildings
June 2016	Axis Bank	US$500 m*	2.88	5	Climate Bonds Standard	Renewable energy, low carbon buildings and transport
Aug 2016	ReNew Power	INR5.0 billion	n/a	n/a	Climate Bonds Standard	Renewable energy
Aug 2016	NTPC	INR20 billion*	7.38	5	Climate Bonds Standard	Renewable energy
Aug 2016	Greenko	US$500 m*	4.88	7	Sustainalytics	Renewable energy
Dec 2016	YES Bank	INR3.3 billion	7.62	7	n/a	Renewable energy
Feb 2017	ReNew Power	US$475 m*	6	5	Climate Bonds Standard	Renewable energy
Mar 2017	REDA (x2)	INR7.0 billion	8.12 & 8.05	10	Climate Bonds Standard	Renewable energy

Source: "The State of the Market/Update 2017", Climate Bonds Initiative, p. 2, https://www.climatebonds.net/files/files/CB-HSBC-2017-India-Final-01.pdf, accessed September 13, 2018.

Table 4:   Green bond issues (2017).

Issuer name	Issued (US$ million)	Use of proceeds
Greenko Investment co	1,000	Energy
IREDA — Six deals	651	Energy
Azure Power Energy	500	Energy
Indian Railway Finance Corp	500	Transport
Rural Electrification Corp	450	Energy
Power Finance Corp	400	Energy
Jain International Trading	200	Energy, Water, Adaptation
L&T Infrastructure Finance Company Ltd.	103	Energy
Total	3,804	

Source: Country briefing July 2018, India State of the Market Climate Bonds Initiative, p. 2, https://www.climatebonds.net/files/files/INDIA%20country%20briefing_Climate%20Bonds%20Initiative_July%202018%281%29.pdf, accessed October 20, 2018.

Table 5:   Oversubscription proportion by Indian companies.

Company	Oversubscription proportion (%)
Axis Bank	2.2
EXIM Bank	3
REC	3.9
NTPC	1.45
YES Bank	2
Greenko Group	1.5
IREDA (2016)	5.1
IREDA (2017)	1.74
AZURE POWER	2
IRFC	3

Source: "Unlocking the Green Bond potential in India", Energy and Resources Institute, p. 9, http://www.teriin.org/sites/default/files/2018-05/Report%20under%20NFA%20grant_2018.pdf, accessed October 20, 2018.

oversubscribed 5 times; and in most instances, the issues — as visible from Table 5 — have been oversubscribed usually twice. The capital mobilised as a result of the enthusiastic response is significant as noted from the fact that issues of sizes between US$100–500 million comprise more than 50%

of resources mobilised through green bond issues in India, which has now amounted to more than US$7 billion.[15]

Competitive prices

Prices of renewable energy in India have become remarkably competitive over time. This is largely due to India's success in determining prices through competitive auctions. India's national and state level auctions in renewable energy have driven down prices fast. The latest minimum bid prices for wind and solar energy have been Rs. 2.64/unit and Rs. 2.44/unit, respectively.[16] These are among the most competitive in the world.

Two factors have contributed to the rapid decline in renewable energy prices. The first is the introduction of competitive national and state auctions for bidding energy prices. The auctions have been bringing down prices as energy producers charge lower and lower for long-term power purchase agreements.[17] Along with auctions, as discussed earlier, access to cheaper options for finance such as green bonds, have helped in reducing capital costs and led to lower bid prices. The combined effect of these two factors has been to push solar power prices in India from around Rs. 11/unit in FY2010 to Rs. 2.44/unit in FY2017. The challenge is to maintain the momentum while mobilising finance.

Maintain investment momentum

While lower costs of finance and consequent lower tariffs are good news for consumers, from an investors' perspective, low prices raise concerns over long-term profitability and return on investments from these projects. In the solar power industry, such concerns are now prominent for both larger utility-scale projects and smaller roof-top projects.

The immediate implication of investors developing doubts over long-term returns is growth of anxieties over fates of power purchase agreements they have entered into. These agreements have been subjects of intense discussion in recent years due to the credit and finance getting stuck in infrastructure projects. Progressive drop in power tariffs would encourage consumers to switch between competing energy service providers by reviewing purchase agreements with existing providers and exploring exit clauses. In India, this is increasingly becoming noticeable in the smaller roof-top category of projects being developed for commercial and industrial purposes by renewable energy companies and financed by third-party investors.

The situation is somewhat different for larger utility-scale projects. These projects are supplying power to grids that are providing power to distribution companies for selling onwards to consumers at tariffs fixed by power tariff regulators. Tariffs fixed by the latter are not based entirely on developments in solar power or renewables alone. These are determined on the basis of energy obtained from all sources including fossil-fuel-based sources.

Coal-based electricity comprises almost 60% of the total grid-connected capacity in India. Thus thermal power prices continue to influence overall grid power tariffs. While solar power and renewable prices might be much lower than thermal power prices, the benefits might not get completely passed on to consumers, as prices at which grids sell power to distribution companies would remain relatively higher given the energy-mix. The end-result for solar power developers indicates a somewhat complicated assessment of long-term prospects.

Issues for the Future

The challenge for shifting to a "clean" world depends on abilities of national economies to shift to renewable sources of energy consumption. The role of solar energy is particularly critical in this regard. The International Solar Alliance would be a major initiative in taking the world forward on a clean energy path. India is expected to be a leading actor in the effort.

As the key proponent of the International Solar Alliance and a country focused on making renewable energy the core source of energy needs for more than a billion people, India has come a long way in developing a robust domestic solar power industry. Its experiences are important pointers towards challenges that other developing countries and emerging markets are likely to face in pursuing clean energy goals.

As discussed in this chapter, state support is essential for the development of fledgling renewable energy industries. At the same time, however, such support cannot be forever. In India's case, the support has helped in improving investor confidence. But such support cannot be traded-off for efforts to bring down cost of finance for developing solar power. This is particularly so at a time when the Indian banking sector is suffering from major problems of non-performing loans.

The Indian experience points to the importance of bringing down cost of finance for making renewable energy an affordable option for mass consumption. India suffers from high bank interest rates due to large non-performing loans that its banks have accumulated over time leading to inflexibility of interest rates and insistence on high collaterals. In countries where interest rates are lower, cost of bank finance might be less. But even then, options of going "global" through overseas debt issue like green bonds enables emerging markets to involve the global community and private investors in more meaningful ways in solar power development.

The remarkable success in bringing down solar prices in India points to the necessity of identifying cheap sources of finance and competitive mechanisms for determining prices. But low prices have the downside of influencing investor sentiments. At the same time, they bring for consumers more choices along with legal complications for revisiting power purchase agreements. Whether all these would lead to alterations in financing models with developers shifting to experimental templates with more risks is uncertain. At the same time, price movements, like the ones noted are also likely to reflect in new consumer–producer relations through revised contractual obligations.

The current global public policy challenges in the arena of solar power development present fascinating opportunities for deeper study and research. The issues are diverse including the role of state subsidies, cheaper cost of development finance, mainstreaming green bonds and maintaining investment momentum. India is well poised to offer emerging markets and developing countries several prospective ideas and insights in this regard.

End Notes

1. Article 2c, Paris Agreement, UN 2015; http://unfccc.int/files/essential_background/convention/application/pdf/english_paris_agreement.pdf, accessed October 20, 2018.

2.   'Paris Agreement Ratificiation Tracker', Climate Analytics; https://climateanalytics. org/briefings/ratification-tracker/, accessed October 20, 2018.

3.   International Solar Alliance http://isolaralliance.org/AboutISA.aspx, accessed October 20, 2018.

4.   'India's renewable energy capacity to double by 2022, report says', Hindustan Times, 4 October 2017, https://www.hindustantimes.com/environment/ india-s-renewable-energy-capacity-to-double-by-2022-report-says/story-9YFGwdg1PdHmQTFKLGgDTJ.html, accessed December 5, 2018.

5.   "Energy Statistics 2018 (Twenty Fifth Issue)", Central Statistics Office, Ministry of Statistics and Programme Implementation, Government of India, New Delhi, March 2018, p. 3, http://mospi.nic.in/sites/default/files/ publication_reports/Energy_Statistics_2018.pdf, accessed October 22, 2018.

6.   "Energy Statistics 2018 (Twenty Fifth Issue)", Central Statistics Office, Ministry of Statistics and Programme Implementation, Government of India, New Delhi, March 2018, p11, http://mospi.nic.in/sites/default/files/ publication_reports/Energy_Statistics_2018.pdf, accessed October 22, 2018.

7.   "Energy Statistics 2018 (Twenty Fifth Issue)", Central Statistics Office, Ministry of Statistics and Programme Implementation, Government of India, New Delhi, March 2018, Foreword, http://mospi.nic.in/sites/default/ files/publication_reports/Energy_Statistics_2018.pdf, accessed October 22, 2018.

8.   Ladislaw, Sarah, "Payment Security Mechanism for Solar Power in India: Can India Secure its Future and the Future of Solar Developers as well?" Center for Strategic & International Studies, February 10, 2017, https:// www.csis.org/analysis/payment-security-mechanism-solar-power-india-can-india-secure-its-future-and-future-solar, accessed October 20, 2018.

9.   'India-based Solar IPP Azure Power Raises $500 million Through Bond Sales' cleantechies.com, July 31, 2017; http://cleantechies.com/2017/07/31/ india-based-solar-ipp-azure-power-raises-500-million-through-bond-sales/, accessed October 20, 2018.

10. Issue Paper: Green Bonds in India; USAID, Department of State, United States of America; Ministry of Power, Government of India; Ministry of New and Renewable Energy, Government of India; February 2015.

11. 'Global green bonds set to hit record levels; India to lead emerging markets: Moody's', Business Line, February 7, 2018; http://www.thehindubusi- nessline.com/markets/global-green-bonds-set-to-hit-record-levels-india-to-lead-emerging-markets-moodys/article22677873.ece

12. Unlocking the Green Bond potential in India", Energy and Resources Institute, p8, http://www.teriin.org/sites/default/files/2018-05/Report%20 under%20NFA%20grant_2018.pdf, accessed September 13, 2018.

13. Unlocking the

14. "Unlocking the Green Bond potential in India", Energy and Resources Institute, p 7, http://www.teriin.org/sites/default/files/2018-05/Report%20 under%20NFA%20grant_2018.pdf, accessed September 13, 2018.

15. 'Brown to Green', 2017, Climate Transparency; Page 25; https://newcli-mate.org/wp-content/uploads/2017/06/brown_to_green_report-2017.pdf, accessed October 25, 2018.

16. "Unlocking the Green Bond Potential in India' TERI, p. 9; http://www. teriin.org/sites/default/files/2018-05/Report%20under%20NFA%20 grant_2018.pdf, accessed October 20, 2018.

17. Ministry of New and Renewable Energy, http://mnre.gov.in, accessed October 20, 2018.

18. 'Indian solar prices hit record low, undercutting fossil fuels', The Guardian, May 10, 2017 https://www.theguardian.com/environment/2017/may/10/ indian-solar-power-prices-hit-record-low-undercutting-fossil-fuels, accessed October 20, 2018.

Chapter 11

South Asia's Energy Transition: Key Issues and the Path Ahead

Christopher Len and Roshni Kapur

Introduction

South Asia encompasses eight countries with a population over 1.8 billion, with India alone having a population of over 1.2 billion. These countries face energy security and access issues. Afghanistan is heavily dependent on imported electricity, Bangladesh does not have enough supply of natural gas, Bhutan has no oil and gas reserves, parts of North India have limited electricity supply, the Maldives and Sri Lanka are heavily reliant on liquid fuel, Nepal faces blackouts and power shortages especially in the dry seasons and Pakistan is highly water-scarce. India is in an important phase in its development story where its energy consumption has nearly doubled since 2000, and it is likely to increase further. Its economy is now in its most energy-intensive phase of development where it is facing demand for energy and dealing with challenges of providing affordable energy to its people. Pakistan and Bangladesh are also witnessing robust growths which in turn is increasing their demands for electricity generation. All these countries are major importers of fossil fuels. These countries will need to develop new strategies to ensure energy and fuel availability for their growth.

The region is also highly vulnerable to climate change and environmental degradation. Sri Lanka, the Maldives and parts of Bangladesh are in low-lying areas which makes them susceptible to extreme weather events. Pakistan is deeply water scarce where rising temperatures may make it one of the most water-stressed countries in the world. India meanwhile faces major air pollution problems. Environmental issues such as these have adverse effects in the region such as submerging human settlements, food and water insecurity, and agricultural productivity and health problems.

According to the World Bank, South Asia is an economically dynamic region and it is expected to remain the fastest-growing region in the world in 2019, mainly driven by domestic demand.[1] However, electricity shortages is one of South Asia's most significant barriers to achieve its development.[2] It also pointed out that based on 2016 figures, South Asia has the world's second largest population living off the grid, which translates into an estimated 255 million people, accounting for more than a quarter of all people in the world living without access to electricity.

The report noted that South Asia's three largest economies, India, Pakistan and Bangladesh with a combined population of 1.6 billion, account for 98% of South Asia's electricity supply. These three also have 300 million people living in extreme poverty subsisting on less than US$1.90 a day and 245 million lacking access to electricity.[3] These three key economies remain heavily reliant on fossil fuel and their power sectors alone are said to have "emitted 1.15 billion tons of carbon dioxide for power generation in 2015, almost as much as the power sectors of all the Organisation for Economic Co-operation and Development (OECD) countries in Europe."[4]

Broadly, the World Bank report underscores what the authors in this edited volume have argued, that the region faces a challenge in enabling energy access in the face of growing demand. This challenge is further complicated by today's global agenda on low carbon energy transition, where there is a push for future energy requirements to be met in a sustainable manner that would complement and support economic and social development and environmental protection. While there is a common challenge in enabling energy access, the region being one of the least integrated in the world faces barriers in regional energy cooperation and trade which are largely political in nature due to rivalry and distrust. Other factors such as lack of port infrastructure and poor connectivity have also impeded regional cooperation. This chapter examines the concept of energy transition and how it relates to the key issues covered in this volume and then offers some thoughts on South Asia's low carbon energy transition and finally, the path ahead.

Explaining Energy Transition

While there is a growing recognition on the importance of low carbon energy transition, it also needs to be pointed out that the energy transition pathway and outcome would be based on specific national and local conditions of each country. From a historical perspective, energy transition is usually a slow process as energy systems are not very dynamic, requiring technological breakthroughs, the replacement and transition from old to new energy, and changes to consumption behaviours. From a historical perspective, Vaclav Smil has described the process as "the change in the composition (structure) of primary energy supply, the gradual shift from a specific pattern of energy provision to a new state of energy system".[5] This change is systemic in nature, being intrinsically bound with the political, economic, industrial, social and environmental developments of the country.

A related concept that helps to frame our understanding of the energy transition process is the "energy trilemma". The World Energy Council (WEC) pointed out that governments need to keep in mind the "energy trilemma" which involves balancing *energy security*, *energy equity* and *environmental sustainability*. It defines energy security as the "[e]ffective management of primary energy supply from domestic and external sources, reliability of energy infrastructure, and ability of energy providers to meet current and future demand." Energy equity refers to the "[a]ccessibility and affordability of energy supply across the population." Environmental sustainability "[e]ncompasses achievement of supply- and demand-side energy efficiencies and development of energy supply from renewable and other low carbon sources."[6] This trilemma entails a "complex interwoven links between public and private actors, governments and regulators, economic and social factors, national resources, environmental concerns, and individual behaviours."[7]

Key Issues in South Asia's Low Carbon Energy Transition

Ensuring universal access that is sustainable

Based on the observations of the authors in this volume, it is evident that South Asia's low carbon energy transition efforts remain at an early phase and is often a rocky process. First they would need to cope with rising energy demand in order to facilitate continued economic growth, ensuring universal access to expanding population and rising expectation of the burgeoning middle class. Second, as growing energy consumers and with their heavy reliance on fossil fuels, they would need to ensure that efforts towards universal energy access is also sustainable, which means that they will need to limit their greenhouse gas solutions as well as to address local environmental pollution challenges. This in turn means that the governments would need to invest more in renewable energy sources; whose vast potential remains largely underutilised.

The United Nations Sustainable Development Goal (SDG) 7: Affordable and Clean Energy looks to ensure access to affordable, reliable, sustainable and modern energy by 2030. Specifically, it notes the focus on "universal access to energy, increased energy efficiency and the increased use of renewable energy through new economic and job opportunities is crucial to creating more sustainable and inclusive communities and resilience to environmental issues like climate change."[8] Similarly, the World Bank has noted that access to energy is at the heart of development and this challenge of universal access incudes both poor communities in urban areas, as well as isolated and disbursed communities in rural and remote areas.[9]

In the context of South Asia, while there is recognition that energy access needs to be sustainable, the governments are faced with the short-term pressures in ensuring energy access as a means towards poverty alleviation and the concern is that they would prioritise energy security and energy equity over environmental sustainability. However, this practice is not sustainable environmentally as well as from an economic point of view. To give an example, according to the World Health Organization (WHO) India has 14 out of 20 of the most polluted cities in terms of PM2.5 levels in 2016.[10] Three out of five of the world's most polluted cities listed by WHO in 2018 are in South Asia, namely New Delhi, Mumbai and

Dhaka.[11] This results in serious health effects which in turn affects economic productivity.[12]

Public–private partnerships

The key domestic challenges for the shift towards low carbon energy sources are due to the lack of affordability for communities and financial resources for entrepreneurs, poor planning, coordination and institutional support, the lack of an enabling regulatory framework and poor infrastructure assets. While keeping in mind that objectives and constraints vary depending on location — both between and within countries — there is ample room for public–private partnerships as well as community engagement. This will enable investors and developers to explore various modern clean energy technology mixes, innovative business models and a supportive regulatory framework towards ensuring universal energy access that is at the same time affordable, reliable and sustainable.

There is also a lot more potential for South Asia governments to tap into international funding sources such as venture capital, insurance firms, investment banks and advisory groups. This is especially since private sector investment participation is essential in order for South Asian countries to improve critical energy infrastructure, invest in clean energy solutions and boost shared prosperity. Governments should pay more attention on attracting low carbon funding through foreign investments and rely less on developmental aid. This would require them to develop an investment-friendly environment defined by political stability, security and a robust regulatory environment.

Regional cooperation

In terms of regional energy cooperation, the authors have pointed to various political factors that have impeded integration affecting energy connectivity. At the same time, energy cooperation can be useful in facilitating closer regional ties. There is recognition that regional cooperation can help the South Asian governments achieve better energy security in a sustainable manner. The Asian Development Bank (ADB) has pointed out the benefits of subregional power trades in reducing the need for new power generation plants in each country, noting that such regional power trade and cross-border connections can result in the more efficient use of scarce resources.[13]

As a showcase, ADB pointed to Bangladesh's first cross-border connection with India, completed in 2013, which is also South Asia's first interconnection of two national grids. This enabled Bangladesh to import 500 megawatts of electricity from India. This is a good example of cooperation between countries to address gaps in energy poor areas, in utilising the region's vast and varied energy resources; this ultimately generated economic benefits on both sides as well as improved political goodwill bilaterally. [14]

International energy diplomacy

Beyond regional cooperation on cross-border electricity trading, South Asian governments need to do more strategic engagement in the field of energy diplomacy, by enhancing energy dialogue with energy producing states and regions such as Myanmar, Russia, Central Asia, the Middle East, the United States, Australia, as well as improving collaboration on issues related to energy infrastructure development, technological collaboration on new energy, and capacity building with the clean energy leaders from European Union, Japan and China. India's membership into the International Renewable Energy Agency in 2009 and its decision to join the International Energy Agency as an Association country in 2017 are examples of positive steps to enhance India's energy governance standing, and improve its collaboration network at the global level.

India's participation in the China-initiated Asian International Investment Bank also demonstrates the benefits of collaboration despite New Delhi's wariness towards China's Belt and Road Initiative and Beijing's agenda on regional connectivity and infrastructure projects. India was the top borrower from AIIB in 2017 for infrastructure projects worth US$1.5 billion[15] and remained the "biggest commitment country" for AIIB in 2018.[16] The first loan to India was US$160 million to strengthen the power transmission and distribution system in the State of Andhra Pradesh. According to AIIB, this project was funded in support of the Government of India's Power for All program that was launched in 2014 to provide an efficient, reliable and affordable electricity supply to all consumers across selected states within 5 years from the start of implementation of the programme in each state.[17] Subsequently on September 27, 2017, it provided US$100 million to cofinance with ADB, which provided US$50 million, a transmission system strengthening project in the State of Tamil Nadu.[18]

Besides India, AIIB also provided energy project funding to Bangladesh (3 projects)[19] and Pakistan (1 project)[20] which shows the importance of development finance for South Asia. These developments represent a step in the right direction as they demonstrate how given the right conditions of enhanced transparency and multilateral inclusiveness, investments in the South Asian energy sector does not have to be burdened with poor governance and corruption, or be viewed through the lens of zero-sum geostrategic rivalry.

Conclusion — The Path Ahead

This conclusion briefly sums up this chapter but it can also serve as a final conclusion for this this edited volume. It is noted that South Asian developing countries, with India being the largest, are entering their most energy-intensive phase of economic growth. The South Asian governments understand the importance of ensuring sufficient energy supply as a key criteria for national development. However, they also realise that their energy demand cannot be met entirely through domestic sources. Regional cooperation is an important way for the countries to meet their energy security requirements. Meanwhile, their populations have growing expectations with regards to access to modern energy services and better quality of life which includes improving the environment and reducing local pollution.

The region's low carbon energy transition efforts remain at an early phase and is often a rocky process. Ultimately, the success of South Asia's low carbon energy transition will depend on a number of factors namely, the ability to capitalise on energy technological advancements, the acceptance of the need to balance energy security, energy equity and environmental sustainability in facilitating energy access, having the right investment environment to encourage public–private partnerships along with the ability to attract low carbon funding through foreign investments with less reliance on developmental aid, and finally, greater intraregional and international collaboration in the spirit of shared prosperity.

End Notes

1. World Bank, South Asia overview, Updated October 5, 2018, http://www.worldbank.org/en/region/sar/overview, accessed December 1, 2018.
2. Fan Zhang, *In the Dark: How Much Do Power Sector Distortions Cost South Asia?* (Washington DC: World Bank, 2019).
3. *Ibid.*
4. *Ibid.*
5. Vaclav Smil, *Energy Transitions: History, Requirements, Prospects* (Santa Barbara, CA: Praeger, 2010), p. vii.
6. World Energy Council, *World Energy Trilemma Index 2018*, (London: World Energy Council, 2018), p. 9, https://trilemma.worldenergy.org/reports/main/2018/2018%20Energy%20Trilemma%20Index.pdf, accessed December 1, 2018.
7. World Energy Council, *Energy Trilemma*, https://www.worldenergy.org/work-programme/strategic-insight/assessment-of-energy-climate-change-policy/, accessed December 1, 2018.
8. United Nations Sustainable Development Goals, Goal 7: Affordable and Clean Energy, https://www.un.org/sustainabledevelopment/energy/, accessed December 1, 2018.
9. "Access to Energy is at the Heart of Development," *World Bank*, April 18, 2018, https://www.worldbank.org/en/news/feature/2018/04/18/access-energy-sustainable-development-goal-7, accessed December 1, 2018.
10. "14 out of world's 20 most polluted cities in India: WHO," *Indian Express*, 2 May 2018, http://www.newindianexpress.com/nation/2018/may/02/14-out-of-worlds-20-most-polluted-cities-in-india-who-1809107.html Accessed 01 December 2018.
11. Simon Roughneen, "Two-thirds of all air pollution deaths occur in Asia", Nikkei Asian Review, May 2, 2018, https://asia.nikkei.com/Economy/Two-thirds-of-all-air-pollution-deaths-occur-in-Asia, accessed January 17, 2018.
12. Iain Marlow, "The World's Fastest-Growing Economy has the World's Most Toxic Air," *Bloomberg*, October 22, 2018, https://www.bloomberg.

com/news/features/2018-10-21/the-world-s-fastest-growing-economy-has-the-world-s-most-toxic-air, accessed December 1, 2018.

13. "Regional Cooperation in the Energy Sector," *Asian Development Bank*, undated, https://www.adb.org/sectors/energy/issues/regional-cooperation, accessed December 1, 2018.

14. "First India-Bangladesh Power Interconnection Feeds Greater Access to Electricity," *Asian Development Bank*, December 7, 2017, https://www.adb. org/news/videos/first-india-bangladesh-power-interconnection-feeds-greater-access-electricity, accessed December 1, 2018; "Bangladesh-India Electrical Grid Interconnection Project: South Asia's First Interconnection of Two National Grids," *Knowledge and Power: Lessons from ADB Energy Projects* (Manila: Asian Development Bank, 2015), p. 86.

15. "India a top borrower from China-sponsored AIIB in 2017," *The Economic Times*, January 11, 2018, https://economictimes.indiatimes.com/news/ economy/finance/india-a-top-borrower-from-china-sponsored-aiib-in-2017/articleshow/62461954.cms, accessed December 1, 2018.

16. "India biggest commitment for AIIB: Official," The Hindu, November 1, 2018, https://www.thehindubusinessline.com/economy/macro-economy/ india-biggest-commitment-for-aiib-official/article25390128.ece, accessed December 1, 2018.

17. "AIIB Approves First Loan to India for $160 million to Support Power Sector," May 3, 2017 https://www.aiib.org/en/news-events/news/2017/ 20170503_001.html, accessed December 1, 2018; India: Andhra Pradesh 24 × 7 — Power For All — Project Description, *Asia Infrastructure Development Bank*, May 2, 2017 https://www.aiib.org/en/projects/ approved/2017/india-andhra-pradesh.html, accessed December 1, 2018.

18. India: Transmission System Strengthening Project — Project Description, *Asia Infrastructure Development Bank*, September 27, 2017, https://www. aiib.org/en/projects/approved/2017/india-transmission-system.html, accessed December 1, 2018.

19. Bangladesh Bhola IPP, *Asia Infrastructure Development Bank*, February 9, 2018, https://www.aiib.org/en/projects/approved/2016/bangladesh-distribution-system.html, accessed December 1, 2018; Bangladesh: Distribution System Upgrade and Expansion Project — Project Description, *Asia Infrastructure Development Bank*, June 24, 2016, https://www.aiib.org/ en/projects/approved/2016/bangladesh-distribution-system.html, accessed December 1, 2018, Bangladesh: Natural Gas Infrastructure and Efficiency Improvement Project, *Asia Infrastructure Development Bank*, March 22,

2017, https://www.aiib.org/en/projects/approved/2017/bangladesh-natural-gas-infrastructure.html, accessed December 1, 2018.

20. Tarbela 5 Hydropower Extension Project — Project Description, *Asia Infrastructure Development Bank*, September 27, 2016, https://www.aiib.org/en/projects/approved/2016/pakistan-tarbela-5.html, accessed December 1, 2018.

CPSIA information can be obtained
at www.ICGtesting.com
Printed in the USA
BVHW042357150719
553541BV00008B/73/P